Gabriel Ramirez
65 Morton St 4K
NY NY 10014

#8C
NYORK. NY. 10001

wart Shining
Spring St. #
w York, NY

Stephanie Rein
110 Riverside Dr. Ap
New York, NY 10024

DAYTON'S

January 20, 2010

Dear Thomas,
   II brought my copy of
American Modern up to Litchfield
this past weekend and read the
chapters on Wealthily and Fifth
Avenue at the table in front of
the bay window in the living room
   It was a beautiful

THOMAS O'BRIEN

AERO

THOMAS O'BRIEN

AERO

Beginning to Now

Written with Lisa Light

ABRAMS New York

For Laura and Danny

ARTFUL ROOTS

LEAP OF FAITH

Oftentimes over the years I have been asked what, exactly, is Aero.

Here is the simplest answer: Aero is a studio and a store. Two connected businesses coexisting under one roof.

But I could also say that Aero is a laboratory. It is a location in the downtown neighborhood of Soho, in New York City. For some, it is a place to go for ideas about design as much as to shop.

People come to know Aero in different ways. Sometimes visitors to the store don't realize that Aero is at all related to the designer Thomas O'Brien, even though I am the proprietor and am in the studio every day. Sometimes people who know of my work wander in or otherwise learn that I have a store and then become customers. Sometimes store customers turn into clients of the studio for interior projects.

A store is by nature an outgoing business, while I am a shy, reserved person. I always say that Aero has taught me how to have a public side.

Aero is a constant imagined experiment.

As of this writing, it is twenty years old.

And now it is the subject of this book.

I have wanted to create a book about Aero for a number of reasons. In many ways Aero represents the through-line between my own style of design and the individual character of the projects I design for clients. I have a place where I can create a collection and an environment that are closest to my interests at any given time; but those ideas are always up for interpretation and can be changed to suit the customers who take them home. These ends—work and home, product and interior design, store and studio—are all mutually present here and they continually cross-pollinate.

This is a book about a creative process and the ideas that have come out of putting together a store over the years. Though there are some interiors to consider, the book is really about ingredients: the items and themes that go into creating a space, the details and materials used, a close-up way of looking at design.

And this is also a book about photography as a memory keeper. Because along with the constant flux of items that have passed through Aero's doors over twenty years, there has grown a very large archive of photography that we've used primarily to document all those things—so many moments from the store, all the way back to its very beginnings, which make this portrait both personal and possible.

Much of the photography in the book hasn't ever been published and wasn't really meant to be. These are the behind-the-scenes snapshots that we took to record the work in progress, to capture a detail or a feeling. There are grainy store images and album photos of my early homes. Some of the pictures are very unproduced, though I think they are more magical and innocent and of their time for being so. I've also included a reminiscent sampling of all the furniture and objects that we've photographed for customers and our records. My staff and I have taken thousands of product

pictures over the years; and these we have always tried to compose nicely and elegantly, though perhaps not always of equally perfect quality, to reflect the character of Aero in our sales memos.

Still, in this time of increasingly idealized images of designed living and quick clicks online that keep us focused on the present, I like the fact that I can look back on these imperfect pictures and see not only what was there, but what was really happening.

Making this book also allows me to share Aero as the singular experience it is. In the face of mass media and the vast franchising of so many brands, I sense that there may never be a more relevant time to advocate for the opposite and more intimate way of being a merchant and designer. I choose for Aero to stay small and special as a destination. I've come to know the people I work with as a family (and I'll introduce some of them here). I think there is a necessary depth to human interaction in design, and one needs a place where things can be touched, examined, and explained. These ideas have always driven Aero to be one very unique world that you can still walk into, six days a week.

I offer this book as a real chronicle of the joys and preoccupations of running a store, and the influences that find their way into my studio and out into friends' and clients' homes. This is a book about work, not illusion. I hope that traveling back to the beginning and sharing these memories with me will have its own poetry. After all, I opened Aero to have a place to work on and be among things that I love every day. It's my leap of faith. It's what I always come back to.

SOHO

Soho was really the only neighborhood that I ever considered for Aero. It was the New York I knew, familiar from my college years at the Cooper Union, even more than the East Village, which is

closer to the school. Like many students, I didn't live in the East Village. First I lived briefly on the Upper West Side and then far west in Soho on Renwick Street. From Cooper Square I'd walk south down Broadway and across Prince Street to go home. At that time there weren't many neighborhood shops in Soho, but Prince Street was where the small local grocery and deli were. So, that was my route, every day. Wherever I've lived in New York, from West Soho to East Sixtieth Street to West Fifty-Seventh, I've thought daily of downtown.

In the 1980s my friends and I went to Soho after school for the galleries, for the early little Tibetan shops, for global stores like Craft Caravan, and the Indonesian furniture importers operating out of old factory loft spaces. I went for the old commodity stores on Broadway, the odd ramshackle shops and outdoor clothing markets on Houston Street. I still have coats and vintage hunting shirts and jackets from some of these places; I still use so much of this material even today in textile and pattern design. And in the early days, there was a string of wonderful proprietor-run antique shops on the west end of Broome Street that I would visit. Once a month I'd go with friends to Fanelli's for a hamburger. For a time I worked for a painter on Leonard Street in Tribeca and during school I also worked on and off at the Leo Castelli Gallery on Greene Street, doing show installations and other studio tasks. That was the Soho of the art world, when the galleries were arriving on the scene, and artists were the primary settlers of the neighborhood, living and working in their industrial lofts.

Loft living was still exotic and for outliers then. But the concept of the loft was transforming, and with it Soho, in ways full of excitement but also loss and displacement.

When I came back to Soho to open Aero in the 1990s, a different group of residents was moving into those lofts and beginning to hire designers to turn them into much more finished interiors. This was the start of a long decade of gentrification, though the wave of people migrating to Soho was at that point, by and large, still connected to the arts. Those were the people who became our first clients.

Aero's first address, at 132 Spring Street, was a handsome Art Deco brick building. It was an unusual sight in the midst of the older, industrial, cast-iron buildings all around it. The building was only two stories tall, the result of a fire in the 1930s and a subsequent renovation in the 1970s of the surviving floors. I liked that it stood out in the neighborhood. The second floor had been rebuilt with new plain anodized aluminum windows spanning the length of the building, like a glass box. This is the space that became Aero.

The name I came up with and wanted: a shorthand of the word aeroplane, an evocation of the Machine Age that I loved in the city. A word of the future, sounding of air and direction. It was something abstract that was more than just surnames on the shingle of a design firm. The unexpected location of the store and the modernity of this name gave Aero its identity from the start.

This was to be a physical home for a business, not just a business that dealt in home. Aero was the laboratory for ideas I was working on, in a neighborhood still somewhat off the beaten path; it was a place to be discovered and it remains that today.

The Soho of Aero's beginnings is again changing and disappearing. The art galleries and many of the old shops are gone, making way for new businesses: hotels and restaurants, more fashion and luxury boutiques. We, too, have changed and grown. In 2004 Aero moved to a different, larger space, on Broome Street, east of Broadway. Aero is now one of the few veteran stores that has stayed open in Soho into this new decade; but it is also once again an outpost for a new generation of customers, who stop in when they come shopping downtown.

Lately I've been thinking about what Aero will evolve into next. What will change and what will remain the same? At this point in my life, I am beginning to explore farther afield, and I like the idea of letting the store wander a bit in my imagination, too, as it should after all this time. I'm certainly one to be loyal to this enterprise and to want to preserve it and make it last, just like I do with the people of Aero, our clients, antiques, or even a house. I hold on to Soho still and to this history of a unique store in New York City, but I am always looking for new avenues that will innovate and surprise.

Every day for so long, I've come downtown to this neighborhood I love, and the instinct to create a business in a place and out of the things I care for is no less strong than it was the day I opened Aero. I still believe in what we are doing and in maintaining the local fabric of a city's independent, unusual stores. Even though we have so many voices talking about design in these modern days, that can't replace spaces where things are still made, are still tangible.

So here I stay, with Aero's doors open to the friends and customers who come to find us, where I've put down roots, on the artful edge of the city.

CHAPTER 1

NYC

ON MY OWN

When I look back at the first apartment I had on my own in Manhattan in New York City, I realize that I was aware, even then, of how special a place it was for me. It was a time of so many firsts, filled with good memories, developments, and discoveries.

During this time, around 1989, I had just purchased my first house, a small 1928 Dutch Colonial in Brookhaven Hamlet on Long Island. I really thought of the house as my home base, but I was still working in the city during the week in Creative Services at Polo Ralph Lauren, and I needed a place to live in Manhattan.

I found this one-bedroom rental apartment in a fifth-floor walk-up on East Sixtieth Street, on a very nice block known for its antique stores and the restaurant Serendipity. At that time this area of the Upper East Side was filled with antique shops, of European furniture especially, much more than the antique stores on Bleecker Street in Greenwich Village or other downtown concentrations of dealers. It was a neighborhood I worked in and knew. The apartment was a modest little space with simple old moldings and a marquetry floor that made it charming. I loved the tiny kitchen, which had one of those vintage molded stainless-steel counters with both a sink and a small stove all in one piece.

It certainly all fit into my particular idea of New York living: a small apartment in the city and a house in the country to fix up on the weekends.

My dream had always been to come to New York. I moved here to go to art school at the Cooper Union. And I've always been a collector and a scout, going regularly to all the museums but equally hunting other odd corners of the city for wonderful stuff, blurring the lines between home and school and work. It is in my nature to look to the past, to make compositions out of disparate things, to throw nothing away, and to seek connections of old to new. In school I'd go to Canal Street looking for items for my apartment as much as art supplies for sculpture class. I combed the city the same way for my first little house on Long Island and this brand-new one-bedroom apartment of my own on the Upper East Side. History and historical objects have always had a fascination for me.

In my early career working with the store design team at Polo Ralph Lauren, I kept up this routine. Part of my job was to shop for and seasonally re-create the rooms on the Home Collection floor at the Madison Avenue Polo flagship mansion. This brought me into the world of retail and collecting, finding and sourcing special items for the stores and showrooms in a very substantive way. I had the opportunity to travel in England and Europe, and to learn more about auctions, antiques, and history. I got to meet and work with special vendors and gallerists around New York, who taught me about proper construction and fabrication, and who

became friends. I was exposed to a level of fine and classical and also simple things that inspired me to stretch and try different materials and design ideas at home.

As much as I learned about interiors, what I really completely loved was the world of stores. In many ways my first truly decorated apartment is where I experimented with the ideas that became the basis of my own store a few years later on. This space was the tipping point of my life as an adult in New York. Here, I was interested in creating an urban character that was pared down and modern, my own imagined notion of urbanism—vintage, elegant, and American, not overly formal and European, not stark and aloof. Something more tailored yet still on the spectrum with my 1920s country house and its antiques. I did and still do see myself in this way as an American designer.

In this apartment, I designed and had my first custom upholstery and drapery made. I made my first investments in paintings and photography, choosing unique pieces and framing them in a special fashion. I started to buy finer items that cost a few hundred dollars more than I could really afford, that came out of the locked glass display case in the antique shop or from an auction: white porcelain, Venetian glass, old silver, modernist ceramics, books, timepieces, and vintage astronomy artifacts.

These pieces were the start of a more informed collection that I was beginning for myself, but I see

them as a continuum with earlier finds that I saved from my Cooper Union days and even country auction haunts from when I was a boy. Every stage of my collecting has been fueled by the same instinct to look for beautiful things and stretch myself to learn more; to buy the special one just out of range that I know I'd regret letting go.

In sorting through all the photographs for this book I'm reminded of the particular things that I was gathering together back then. The pictures are objects in themselves, trading back and forth as I did behind the camera with my close friend Laura Resen. Laura and I went to the Cooper Union together, and have been working together in one fashion or another for all of our professional lives. But in these early days, we were just getting started.

I still have so many of these items around me today, even as I continue to edit and refine what I live with. But that is part of what I was learning about collecting in the mixture of that time. We can find possessions and carry them along with us, even as we change and progress. I have always liked the idea of time spent learning and finding, and of creating a collection to be shared that is its own kind of memoir.

In furnishing the apartment I was drawn to natural materials and rich menswear neutrals in browns and cream. And just as I might put together these ingredients in an outfit, so at home I was mixing rustic, modest, and simple things with finer pieces, in easy, changeable layers.

Many of the items in these photos are ingredients that have been ever-constant in the world of Aero. I love this Deco clock especially for its battered charm, and how the face is marred from fifty years or more of clumsy winding. On top of the stack of photos is a favorite picture I took in Paris of my friend Laura Resen, as she is photographing the Nike of Samothrace on its famous landing at the Louvre. Above, a midcentury Murano glass bowl shares a tabletop with a Chinese incense burner. I framed an old photograph of my grandfather on a diving board, from a group of youthful poolside snapshots that were given to me by my grandmother. The mix is personal and collected, saved and found: all parts of the sort of world I look for and enjoy.

My first piece of custom-made furniture was this classic
Chanel sofa, from Jonas Upholstery. Jonas is one of
the workrooms that I've known for my whole career,
and it has always done all of the most special, custom
upholstery for the store. Its version of the Chanel sofa
is one of the truest, nicest interpretations I've seen:
beautifully proportioned, with large, spaced nailhead
trim. I covered mine in Bisonte natural vegetable-tanned
leather. This type of wonderful natural leather was one
of the things I had discovered around this time, through
suppliers that I worked with in the fashion industry.

The Kurt Marcus photograph was one of my first
contemporary art purchases. My cat Emma was a stray
that I rescued outside CBGB on the Bowery when I was
in school, my first pet in New York. Her name came,
curiously enough, from a vintage yard or so of thin,
lettered ribbon that I'd picked up in a junk store. It had
repeated "M"s on it, an elegant, traditional way to label
and sew someone's initials into clothing. A second piece
of ribbon had the letters "TO" and I thought it odd and
magical that together they spelled my name. Emma wore
a piece of the M ribbon as her collar for a long time—a
found identity for a found cat.

When putting together this room, I already had the sofa and desk and I needed a third piece to complete the space. I chose this Indian daybed for that exact spot at the end of the room, almost like a fireplace mantel, a focal point. It was one of the first auction antiques that I'd purchased for myself. I found it at a benefit in Bellport, Long Island; and though I'd seen other pieces like it before, this one had the most handsome aging and unusual greying, spotted color, with iron nailheads and really fantastic, subtle decoration. Later on this became my desk when I opened Aero. The saddle club chair is another piece from Jonas Upholstery.

In the center of the living room, on top of a plain sisal rug, I put an antique Heriz carpet that had belonged to my grandparents, from a group of six or seven carpets that came out of my dad's childhood home. I found them when I was in college, stored away in our family's summer cottage, hidden under the eaves of one of the bedrooms. My dad let me take them, and I still have them all today. This one was my favorite for the blues in it, with brown and just a little bit of red—just a beautiful pattern.

One of the least attractive things about this apartment was the window wall in the living room, with a conspicuous air conditioner, and to be honest, the spot where I kept the cat-litter box hidden. I had an idea to make one long continuous drape that would cover all that, on a slender brass rod with simple hidden flanges that held it to the wall. While working at Polo I had come across this beautiful, lightweight, Japanese habutae silk, which was a fashion fabric really, intended for elegant womenswear. I designed three ceiling-to-floor, softly pooled panels to open at the two windows, covering the whole wall in this translucent silk drapery that illuminated the room. I also made up this type of drapery rod for my bedroom. For that space I chose cream wool challis that I still regularly use in design projects today, especially in modern residences.

Even in the city I was inclined to treat this area just inside the entry like a piece of a country mudroom, with its various shoes and hats and collections. The molding here is original to the apartment. I quite like the look of the simple paneled detail it creates, and have recycled this idea in a number of ways over the years in different residences. I bought the Rodin lithograph on the same trip to Paris where I took the photo of Laura at the Louvre. The books are a set of Shakespeare volumes that I tied together in a stack with twine. They're still tied exactly that way today in the upstairs hallway of my house.

This set of English diaries is from the early 1900s. There are almost thirty years recorded in these beautiful small books that are all identical in size, with dark red or green leather bindings and gilded edges to the paper. When I found them, I so appreciated that these special, preserved, obviously cared-for artifacts had been kept together for almost a century.

I made all the patchwork velvet pillows around the apartment myself, out of scraps of Brunschwig & Fils Tiger and Leopard silk velvet that I collected from the upholsterer. For some, I saddle-stitched narrow strips together in diagonal and straight seams, and then assembled those strips to make one bigger piece of fabric. I actually prefer the patchwork effect that I ended up with. I was using something luxurious in an easy and casual way.

The desk by the kitchen was also something that I put together myself, with a crude old folding table stand that I found in the garage of my Brookhaven house. I had a piece of glass cut with holes drilled along the ends, which attached to the table with fine, round-head, slotted brass screws. By the early 1990s I was seeing different kinds of glass-topped tables with sawhorse and trestle bases in chrome or nickel. This was my take on that look, with a much more rustic, rusty table base and something more industrial to the gadgetry attaching the glass to it.

For years I paired the desk with this Mission chair that I upholstered in deerskin with nailhead trim. That chair is as solid as can be, but with its delicate heft and curves it also looks to me like a modern French Deco antique. I like that odd juxtaposition of American craft with such a European shape, the chance outcome of one chair's design.

In my clothes closet I hung a piece of art that I made and presented in a sculpture class when I was at the Cooper Union. At the time, I was experimenting with appropriating text and pictures. I would tear small squares of print or photography, mostly out of the *New York Times*, always around the same size, and glue one fragment to the center of each page in a notebook. This page came from a Buccellati ad, I remember. For me it was about the beautiful, graphic typography and the elegant charm of the list. I've always loved it, and even as I've collected lots of other art, it's a piece that remains important to me. I've kept it all these years, and it still hangs with my clothing in my current apartment.

When I moved into this apartment I brought the long, low cubby bookcases with me for the bedroom. I'd originally found them on the street when I was in school. They were just these simply made, long rectangular cubbies, and I painted them off-white to hold all my design magazines. Now, I sort through my magazines and keep just tear sheets, except for *The World of Interiors*, which I don't ever seem to tear apart.

CHAPTER 2

STAIRS

BROOKHAVEN

Aero is often described as having a city aesthetic, but it has always been influenced by my interests and time in both the city and the country. These places represent to me two sides of my life, one about work and the other about rest. The city is stimulating and extroverted, while the country is slower and restorative. When I am out at my house on Long Island, I have the time to be more domestic. I garden, cook, and keep house. I am quiet. I putter. I recharge.

Of course, these experiences don't have to be divided into separate homes. But in my life, especially having grown up in a rural place, the opportunity to know two distinct locales in which I spend time helps me continually see and braid together the opposing realities we all deal with at home. In the work I've done over the years, the question has been how to find a balance between the two. I've tried to find each place's aspects in the other, to create a feeling of retreat and also a place of productivity, regardless of where the compass may point.

I have such fondness for my little house in Brookhaven Hamlet. It was the very first place that I chose and bought myself, all on my own. The cottage had natural shingles, with a fire-engine-red door and a Dutch gambrel roof covered in 1940s green hexagonal asphalt tiles. It was turned on an angle toward the street on a semi-circular drive, rather than facing straight on like the other houses lined up tidily around it. Not long after I bought the house, someone stopped me in the Village and told me that I shouldn't ever change the color of the door, because people used it as an informal marker on their way to the marina; in the way of

small towns, everyone always just said to go to the end of the road past the cottage with the red door. Today the house has been renovated, but it truly was this idyllic local landmark for many, many years, and of course, in my time there, I always kept the red door.

On the property, there was also a garage building with old sliding barn doors, and between the house and the garage, the small yard had an enormous old-growth maple tree. Probably when the house was built that tree must already have been quite large. I loved it and thought of it as my tree. To have a yard and a garden and trees to tend speaks to a whole different part of me that comes from being raised in upstate New York. And so the outdoors and the indoors here were an equal pair to me. I've always spoken of this place as my little house with the big tree.

This Brookhaven cottage is in a kind of memory lineage with my grandmother's home in Hamilton, New York, where I first gained an appreciation for the civility of old houses and saw the translation of classical architecture and antiques into a simpler American style. There is always that difference, too, when dealing with a freestanding house—the autonomy, the surrounding yard or landscape instead of buildings and apartments layered one on top of another. You just see space differently.

And just as my city apartments all grew and progressed out of one another, I couldn't have envisioned my current house on Long Island, nor all the design evolutions that home has brought to my work, if I hadn't had the Brookhaven house first. I miss it still.

What I learned in Brookhaven, I apply to all my work. It is about using old yet beautifully formed things in a clean, modern, edited way. The wonderful, traditional, very pure American carpentry of this nicely crafted little 1920s building had its own beauty and utter simplicity. And while I had things here that were fine and collected, I was also choosing American country and folk objects with a geometry and natural form that were, to me, just as beautiful and chic. The simplicity of these golden objects makes them modern even when they're old or humble. That is the point of view I was making my own here. And it remains in the kind of objects I buy for Aero even today.

I still see myself walking through the fire-engine-red door. The dining room that had to be my first all-purpose room—library, workroom, and eating space all around one table. That kind of table became a symbol to me and has been a staple in numerous homes I've designed since. The green walls I painted, classic yet also modern. The ideal college reading room Venetian blinds. All are ingredients that I've revisited many times over, using them even in the most formal, glamorous New York apartment houses.

I remember how much it meant to me to have a slender old set of stairs to climb; how they turned with a tiny landing under the gambrel roof and then again into a small hallway to reach my two little rooms upstairs. After living in so many walk-up apartments, it is still striking to me just how important having my own set of stairs was. The upstairs and downstairs of this cottage made it a home in a way that a ranch house wouldn't have.

It's funny the things that we long for in a house to call our own. Stairs. A fireplace. A mudroom. Working in the kitchen in the late afternoon sun. They must be part of a collective memory that has to do with comfort and ritual. The style of the rooms can and does change, but the behavior they contain, the ways of coming and going, that is what makes me know I'm at home.

When I look at the early pictures of my house in Brookhaven, I do find modern things and a modern point of view in the photographs themselves. Even though this was a shingled cottage filled with mostly country antiques, the pieces are assembled with an order and style that brings them forward. The house was about fitting together found and older things through their proportion, their natural color, or their shape, and letting each one pause and be so specific and simple. I think that felt fresh and new for that time. A modern sensibility is as much about this notion of composition as the date on an item. Traditional and humble things can be revisited in an edited, individual way that has always seemed right to me.

The two-drawer American mahogany work table stands again at the front door of my current house on Long Island. The photograph above it is a small platinum print of the countryside in Italy, by Laura Resen. During school we both were making small, vintage-feeling photos like this, especially of landscapes. That was very much an art student inclination, to work on this type of atmospheric little print, even when our photography teachers were always trying to convince us to make bigger pictures.

From the time I first explored Brookhaven and the surrounding beachside villages, and bought this first house, it's been special for me to live near the ocean on Long Island. I've always felt pulled by the moods and beauty of that coastline. My affection for it led me to collect hand-colored, early twentieth-century photographs of seascapes. On my mantel I kept a favorite, called *Surf at Pinnacle Rock*, in front of a soft, old sepia-toned picture of a river valley. I left the photo in its original frame with its warm, yellowed mat. I am continually drawn to that color of old paper and parchment, and I love the narrowness of old frames like this. I am forever trying to get framers to do more of this type of completely simple, thin, vintage profile. Above, a graphic, black-and-white Jean Cocteau booklet and a few modernist novels from art school.

I've always liked the classic wood Venetian blinds that you find in early twentieth-century colleges and reading rooms. They seem elegant and masculine and so perfectly vintage to me. This house marks the first time I invested in good, handcrafted ones, made in this exacting way, with wood slats and fabric tape. I bought them for every window on the whole first floor, as one complete idea.

In the dining room, an antique herbarium hangs against a deep, stony green wall: a forerunner of the dark walls to come at Aero. Classic Hitchcock chairs and an ebonized turned-wood pedestal make modern silhouettes around an old desk that I used as the dining table. On the table, an original edition of the Futurama exhibit book from the 1939 World's Fair. An ironstone bowl; a Wedgwood transferware platter of stylized sepia peonies.

CHAPTER 3

AIR

OPENING AERO

Aero opened for business in the fall of 1992. I took many of these pictures just moments before our opening party, on the evening of October 21st. Looking back now, the store looks like itself, like many people's idea of Aero, glowing and peaceful. But there was a very considered process behind putting the space together and, before that, an interesting path that led to the possibility of this store at all.

In the years leading up to Aero, when I was working for Ralph Lauren, Ralph used to tell me, "You've got the merchant bug."

It's true: To be a merchant is certainly its own kind of calling. The job is about forever making attachments, and at the same time letting things go. You are building a thing that is constantly disappearing. I realize the irony in this since I never really give up anything at home. But as a merchant you are always looking ahead for what is next. You are stubbornly saving things and waiting for their time. And you are perpetually inventing a stage, a brand, or a store where these things can exist in a world of their own.

I loved working for Ralph. For a long time, I felt I'd always stay with Polo. Still, his observation solidified into something of a piece of advice over time. A store, especially an independent one, is a world of interest unto itself. And discovering those worlds, even creating one for myself: it's why I came to New York to go to art school, and it's what goes into the work of what I do in design.

It's always been in my nature to be different, to try my own way. I think on some level I did imagine that one day I would have a store of my own.

So when I ultimately left Polo, what I had in mind was not just design, but also a store. At first I had a few small interior design projects, and on some of them I did a bit of work with Bill Sofield, who had also been at Polo.

Bill had initially come to Polo to do architectural work and renovation on store projects, and it was there we became friends. As I moved on from store design to work with Ralph on his homes, Bill and I continued to overlap and follow what the other was up to. Bill had his own new studio at that time. Eventually I called him to help with the architecture and contracting on a house that I was doing in the Hamptons. After that we just naturally began collaborating in the world of homes and interiors.

We were friends who were both just starting out, and we decided to start a business together. This is how Aero originally came into being.

AERO

The idea at the heart of Aero was to create a design store that anyone could visit, open six days a week— not a by-appointment trade showroom, or the specialized world of an art gallery, but something in between and more accessible. There would be antiques, furniture, lighting, table accessories, and art; things European, American, Japanese, and Chinese; city and country influences; objects rustic and classical, bold and delicate, known and unknown. And this collection of things would exist in a kind of evolving modern loft, at the top of a flight of stairs, beyond a striking foyer and balcony.

The design and fabrication of the store—its architecture, balcony, colors, drapery, carpets, and finishes—was itself one of the initial projects of the new Aero studio. With the big expenditures to build the space and produce key store furnishings, much of the merchandise that is seen in these first pictures literally came out of my own house and apartment. Other special antiques came on loan. Richard Kazarian was one antique dealer whom I had known throughout my years at Polo. He had such a magical eye, and he gave us some beautiful European pieces for the opening. Then there were the tabletop objects that I bought from artisan companies that I found at gift fairs. That's continued to be the mix in the store: antiques; vintage, modern, and custom furniture; art and special housewares. Some items from the very beginning, such as our Japanese zinc vases, are classics now that I've been reordering for the store all these years.

For the opening, we had what we had. The space was underfilled, both by design and by the realities of what we could then afford to put in a big open loft. That spaciousness and the air around each grouping ended up becoming an idea about how a store or a home could look spare and composed but not empty or austere—not minimalist at all. Every item was handcrafted and handpicked; ornate details shared space with worn patinas and relaxed layers of objects. The furniture was comfortable and usable. The spareness there is in Aero's beginnings feels elegant and purposeful. It feels modern, quiet, and easy.

Aero has always straddled double worlds—a studio and a store; modern and traditional; permanence and change—and at the beginning it had two voices. Bill and I have often been described in counterpoint, both stylistically and characteristically. Our collaboration lasted only about three years, but short as this was, it was important to both of us. We shared an idea about returning to a certain modern elegance in design and reviving the fellowship of earlier salon days in a public gallery space. It didn't matter at the time that we were inexperienced and unknown, or that the economy of the early 1990s was in a recession. We saw an opportunity to start something new and tried

it. Aero is still the keeper of those intentions, even though our business partnership came to an end.

For me, Aero's opening night and the weeks that followed were full of the butterflies of sharing this big new project that I had been working on for some time. Even today, there is this constant fascination for me in keeping Aero going, keeping it fresh and relevant as a design venue. The merchant in me is still working, not only to find and assemble pieces that I am interested in, but also to create an interesting, authentic, inviting place in which to show them. And then to break it down and do it a different way. Again and again. It's an endless creative exploration. It's why I love having a store.

I took many of these pictures in the minutes just before our opening party. I remember running around the gallery, all of a sudden a New York merchant but still feeling like an excited art student with my camera. At heart I am still always trying to find the art in everything I do.

The habutae silk drapes that I first made for my apartment inspired walls of the same silk drapery at Aero. In fourteen-foot columns that wrapped around the space, the drapes were first of all an elegant way to cope with the huge and unremarkable anodized aluminum windows that had been part of this building's 1970s renovation. But what I loved about them was the beautiful glow that they had, and the way they billowed and moved, with something of a cinematic, old Hollywood feeling. When the drapes were closed, they had the effect of softly backlighting the furniture; other times we would open them to let the views of Soho and the city in. They very quickly became one of Aero's signature features and an element that I've used in a number of client interiors.

Even though the cloth was not too expensive in itself, and I was able to buy it directly from the Japanese supplier, I remember it took over 450 yards to make all the drapery, in what seemed like an extravagant investment at the time. A number of years later on, when they were soiled and a bit worn from exposure, I remade the drapes in a new color, a pale lavender blue, in the same habutae silk.

The studio offices were built into the interior of the loft so that we could save more natural light for the store. In these pictures you can see the over-height paneled and antiqued mirror doors that led to our conference room. I have always liked using mirror in this architectural, glamorous, French modern way. Silver, gilding, mirror, and the couture spirit of European furniture are luxuries that were introduced early on and remain key parts of the Aero look today.

The shine and reflection of this special, Art Deco–style, mirrored and silver-leafed vitrine were ever-constant in the store for many years. The piece was tailored and made for that spot and became the first real place of shelving to display collectibles and tableware.

With a big space to furnish but not much furniture to fill it, the only thing to do at the start of the store was to bring in my furniture from home—both city and country. I placed my Chanel sofa from the apartment in the corner, along with my Mission chair and some of my hand-sewn Tiger Velvet pillows spotted here and there. Other fine pieces came on consignment, like the Italian neoclassical chairs from my friend, antique and art dealer Richard Kazarian. We added some industrial and found things that were purely sculptural and modern, like the hoop skirt form on an anonymous midcentury galvanized metal console.

The Noguchi lanterns have been a favorite at Aero since the beginning. They have such a wonderful simplicity and glow. Benjamin Moore 992 was the color of the store—an atmospheric, earthy taupe background that we added, along with the silk drapery and ebonized floors, to make the loft's drab architecture look rich.

Aero has always had a fashion point of view in the style of textiles, leathers, and trimmings that we use. Above, this is the classic Breck Sofa from Jonas Upholstery that came out of my Brookhaven living room. With its characteristic, long, gently sloped rolled arm, I had it covered in natural linen with blind seams and no welting, the most modern, quiet way I could do it. Other pillows for the store were made up with collected vintage woven-metal and appliqué trims. Shearling hides that came from a leather supplier were used whole, as throws. The look was about taking vintage and luxe elements and pairing them with raw, unfinished ones. Even the gilding that was done on simple tray tables was rubbed through in places to the clay, for this mix of embellishment and naturalism.

These very simple tables were originally designed for a client's house in Sagaponack. For the store we had a new pair made, with raw teak bases and large sheets of inset glass notched around the leg. They started out as a surface on which to display accessories. Later the tables moved into our conference room as one long work space. After a time I replaced the glass with grey gloss formica, a material that I like very much in its early modern applications. This is how the tables have remained to this day.

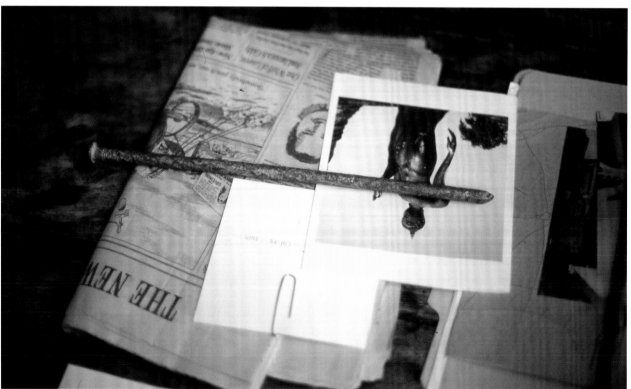

The Indian daybed from my apartment became the desk in my office. Its finish reminds me more of Japanese kiri wood than anything painted, and that grey tone has been a model for many new finishes we've specified over the years at the studio. Small still lifes of objects and piles of test finishes always rotated on the desk. The stylized plaster cameo plaque is one of the few odd things that was actually shoplifted off the wall in the store. I found the rough-hewn roofing nail at Home Depot and used it as a metal finish sample. Above, various hand-painted gesso samples.

I've never been much for filing cabinets, so I refinished a vintage cork and mahogany Paul Frankl sideboard and used that for storage behind my desk. The paint is a favorite stony green neutral; the hardware was re-plated in nickel. The collection on top is a favorite group of long-owned mementos, including a 1930s terra-cotta horse maquette, a color study I did in school, a Jean-Michel Frank lamp that I found just this way, with its paint partially scraped off. I love the charming double meaning of the word Deeds on the nineteenth-century folding document boxes, made in the form of leather-bound books—I've always thought of them as boxes of good deeds.

This vintage botanical chart became the pattern of our Aero tissue paper, with the plant forms in silver ink and the background in different colors over the years. The citron green, pleated silk screen is one of a pair from Sister Parish that I bought for a song at a Sotheby's sale. I found the pair of Chinoiserie chairs as-is, painted in their elusive shade of earthy celadon green, and I have always kept them this way.

CHAPTER 4

CITY COTTAGE

LAURA AT BETHUNE STREET

My friend Laura Resen has always been part of my life in New York. We went to school together, and at different times we've worked on art together. I sell Laura's art at Aero. She photographed my first book. Laura introduced me to some of my first residential clients who are still with me today and she has photographed many of their homes. Between us there are rich varieties and decades' worth of pictures from all of these ongoing collaborations.

In our early years, the subjects of many of these pictures were our own homes. I refer to and use many of the images of these places in my work. They capture certain ideas at their origin point—as each of us was developing our own skill and style—that became part of Aero.

 I imagine Laura's early city homes as representative of who the Aero customer was at the start. I think of her as being there, or even just ahead of the curve, for the moment of an artistic kind of loft living. And I feel there is a modern spirit to Laura's sense of color. Laura's homes are the first places to see the rich mustard, saffron, cinnabar, and orange that are constants for her, and became so for Aero, too. These are colors from the midcentury, but they

are also Eastern, present in her antique Chinoiserie cabinets, in lacquer, and in other accessories.

Laura's style, with its vibrant, warm oranges, represents something different and dynamic that was evolving in this moment. Paired together with Aero's natural tones, and even the soft bit of green in my Brookhaven house, one has the pieces of what I think modern color can be even to this day. So although this book chronicles the history of the studio and the store, I also think it is useful to consider an outside viewpoint, to see where items and ideas from the store went and how people really lived with them and made them their own.

On another level, though I have always made my professional home downtown, it's true that I have mostly lived farther uptown, in the middle of Manhattan actually, near Central Park, and also out on Long Island. But Laura did live downtown, first on Renwick Street in West Soho, in the apartment that I briefly shared with her; next in the West Village; and eventually back in Soho. In many ways she was already of this city and of the world I imagined for Aero, even as early as the time we met at school and only more so as she developed—as a photographer, in her modern personal style, and because of the interesting people she knew.

I didn't design Laura's homes. They are not perfectly renovated worlds, and I love that about them. Laura claimed her spaces with good furniture and art, and worked around the oddities of each apartment she lived in. They are hers and reflect

her wonderful taste. Yet they are also that window onto what an Aero home might have looked like at different points over the years. Most personally, these places are a definite part of how two friends influenced each other. They are populated with our discussions about design: decisions that I helped Laura make, for example, about paint and furniture placement or the framing of art, and things she picked up from the store to mix with her own collected possessions.

And so, Laura's apartments and photographs included in this book are like a parallel timeline for me. I appreciate that certain things I was aiming toward are visible in the generations of a friend's home. They show me her; and in looking back to assemble this book, she shows me what Aero was becoming.

HOME FROM PARIS

The first of Laura's unique New York apartments was on Bethune Street in one of the pretty old corners of the West Village. Laura had the two top floors of a narrow Greek Revival–style townhouse built in 1836, just blocks from the Hudson River and filled with the waterfront's low, tidal, streaming light. The space was like a traditional artist's garret studio with small rooms, a slanted ceiling, and even stairs up to a beamed sleeping attic—almost a tiny cottage in this old part of the city.

To me the Bethune Street space has the same charm and scale as my own small Brookhaven house that I put together during these early years. Both have a modesty that I don't think of as limiting or quaint. Laura's apartment was of another age, but it had the modern energy of something newly formed and fitted together. Her first real, decorated city apartment is not extravagant or huge. It's authentic.

Before she found this spot, Laura left New York for a number of years. After school she worked in Europe and lived in Paris on and off, and she came

home with a bit of the unique, unruffled French sensibility toward modernism and fashion that can make both so chic and easy.

She also came home with some wonderful art and furniture, and books in abundance. Those things were the core of this apartment. Other accessories, lamps, dishes, and furnishings came from visits to Aero. Of vintage pieces over those years, we discovered we had both been collecting the same modern things.

In this Bethune apartment, I see a lifestyle that is cultured but casually elegant. I like that it is not identifiably masculine or feminine. I like the ordered enclosure, the stacks and textures filling up the space. In our homes as in our work, Laura and I would trade ideas back and forth and the oasis of this apartment seems the prototypical version of the kind of interior it is possible to create when starting out with decoration before renovation. I think the majority of homemakers face similar circumstances at one point or another. A full interior design process is not for everyone. But a fresh, charming home doesn't require that.

Though I have always done custom architecture for the clients of my studio, Laura's and my early homes are a reflection of what was happening at Aero and how the look of the store was something that customers might emulate. There might be limitations but also imagination: a belief in bringing small moments into a balance with modern furniture and simple, airy rooms.

Laura had this fantastic nineteenth-century camelback sofa upholstered in mustard yellow wool, along with a pair of classic Aalto bentwood chairs for her living room. I remember talking with her about what color for the walls would work with the yellow sofa and the oranges she liked and with all her vintage Scandinavian blonde wood furniture. A very earthy, rich lichen green, like the color of my dining room in Brookhaven, and also like the world of Aero with its dark walls, served as a foil for both her antiques and the modern furniture. Laura tells me that all these years later, she has heard the room is still painted this same color.

In and among Laura's special collections are various domestic staples from Aero: thick Italian glass dishes, a midcentury seeded glass vase, artisan glass bowls, Aero lamps and trays. When I look at these items from the store's earliest days, I still find myself imagining the different kinds of apartments and houses where they ended up; how they were used, who chose them, what they were mixed with. I like to think that Laura's style gives me a window onto all of that. Her home to me is what the Aero home could be.

Laura favors slim, white, modern framing for a lot of her art. Here at the entrance to the apartment, she grouped several Sonia Delaunay prints that she brought back from her time in Paris. The red painting is by her father, Ken Resen. Ken is an accomplished painter and renowned graphic designer who worked for many years for I. M. Pei. Both he and Laura's mother, Gail, have been wonderful to me over the many years that I've known them. They certainly were part of the enchantment of a thriving artistic New York family when I met Laura at school.

The cinnabar lamp with a vintage silk shade was Laura's find. We often lacquer pieces in that classic red at Aero, and Japanese and Chinese antiques have always filtered through the store, too, in the spirit of things that you might find in many older-school antique shops. But there's also a beauty to be found in the traditional Asian table and cookware that continues to be made. Laura introduced me to the magic of Chinatown and legendary markets like Pearl River in New York, where you can find so many interesting, useful goods that are crafted so nicely even now.

Above right, among the Japanese and Chinese touches in her kitchen, Laura's photo of a Le Corbusier building in France.

Laura truly grew up in the world of midcentury modern design in New York, but she also loves antiques. Both old and modern are here in the library, one of the two small front rooms in the apartment, under the eaves, where she worked. As I remember it, the library table was a section of a neoclassical ebony dining table, while the pair of 1970s Parsons-like straight-back cane chairs came from Aero. I painted them in this shiny pale grey color from the original natural cane; a way of reviving pieces that could otherwise seem dated. Also from Aero is the early Jonathan Adler vase. Aero was one the very first places to sell Jonathan's work when he was starting out as a potter. We commissioned one of his first sets of dishes for a client and we also did some of his earliest lamps together for the store.

The walls of this room were stacked with columns and columns of books. I have always loved this particular picture of all the ivory-toned French volumes. It seems to me a modern way of creating a library, without bookshelves, the books piled high like newspapers, so handsome yet imperfect and casual.

The tiny study right next to the library was Laura's first workroom and office as a photographer in New York. She stored her film in a pair of beautiful antique lacquered Chinese cabinets that she had picked up at the Paris flea markets. To these she added modern pieces in the same striking color—a cinnabar-lacquered Robsjohn-Gibbings desk from Aero; a pair of tomato and ivory molded fiberglass chairs. I love the soft indigo of the carpet here with all the shades of orangey red.

The study has a moody twentieth-century European character. It's the style of old and new that Laura took with her even when she moved on to the modern loft world of Soho. As a designer I continue to be interested in that oldness and the genteel townhouse architecture of places like the West Village; places for artists. And this neighborhood is still enormously charming and very popular today for those same historical and bohemian qualities. Still, so many of its old houses are now expensively renovated and refined, that much of this world is gone. A magical spot like this one, with all of its quirks and corners, is rare to find or afford for one starting out as she was here.

The bedroom at the top of the house, with its original eaves. The ladder leads up to the roof in the common way of old New York lofts. I love the imperial yellow, quilted spread on the bed. The brightness of this open space is a nice gesture after the rich, enclosed rooms with their dark walls downstairs. A Lalique turtle is paired with a Japanese cast bronze one from Aero; we still sell these bronze turtles at the store today.

Laura chose this vintage club chair from Aero. It became the model for one of the first pieces of custom Aero upholstery, called the Geneva chair. I've always returned to this form, with its great proportions and the crisp way that the seat deck and cushion project out from the arm. It is neither too big nor too small. I think the chair may have been leather when I bought it, but I re-covered it in this soft, silver-toned velvet, and I still do like it best in this velvet when we make it even now.

CHAPTER 5

REJUVENATION

BECOMING AERO

If Aero at its opening was the outline of an idea, about interiors and furniture and an eclectic approach to modernism, then its first years in business were the opportunity to color in that picture. As the Spring Street store became known and the studio began to gain more clients, we had more resources, practically speaking, to fill in the blanks.

In the mid-nineties, the store became richer and fuller. It was populated with goods of a higher order, more one-of-a-kind pieces, some with provenance. The spare loft started to feel more like a series of connected rooms.

Looking at pictures of this space now, the materials are visibly more luxurious and chic, including vintage silver, gold leaf, and porcelain. There are more accessories, more lighting, more furniture, and more art. More layers. There is more of a blending of generations between the grace of emerging twentieth-century modernist pieces and the stronger geometry of later modern decades. Most of all I see one of my guiding principles, of older modernism made new. The furniture here refers back to those finer finishes and paler colors from the advent of modernism.

I have always been interested in what earlier pieces might look like if they were made today, out of those pure materials that will develop luster and patina over time. And so this era in the store also marks the inclusion of more of a European modernist look that comes out of what I was adding to my own home and what I was buying for the homes and lofts of the studio's early clients.

The store customers became Aero's first residential clients and, in a way, our muses. Out of their homes grew a mission about furnishing as well as space design. This was the moment to focus on the stuff of what we sold, all the varieties of furniture and goods that would really make up a room. The mid-nineties was the time of modern furniture becoming a collector's item, but also the moment when more frugal versions of star pieces from the auction block were flooding the backs of pickers' trucks, still waiting to be rediscovered, in need of rejuvenation.

I wanted to claim a middle ground between the homes where the wonderful things were not to be touched, and easier rooms assembled out of more casual components. As a shopkeeper I had a mix of things to find, some known, some unknown, some low, some high. I had a thought to buy for the home as an investment in art and furniture that would be collectible but also livable.

I think on this spectrum we were coming up with something of a softer mix, still modern but genuinely pretty, and increasingly genuine.

As part of this direction, the store began refurbishing vintage furniture in special ways. This has become an Aero tradition, to reinvent less significant pieces with a much more hand-picked set of finishes and materials. I bought examples of 1920s neoclassical furniture in mahogany or oak, the kind of cabinetmaking that is honorably crafted yet easily forgotten. And I bought modern factory furniture of the 1940s and '50s by designers like Russel Wright, Heywood Wakefield, James Mont, Paul Frankl, and Paul McCobb, all handsomely designed yet fated to be ubiquitous. But I was not after a pure restoration. I wanted to alter the pieces in a novel way that would let each one be seen as unique.

Besides these pieces to refurbish, I also looked for more individual furniture from the turn of the twentieth century. There is a world of striking woodwork and metal from the 1910s and '20s that needs no reinvention at all. I have always cared for these older gems that were made on the cusp of change, straddling traditional and modern styles, improved by patina and wear. I think that age can be even more intriguing than the mint vintage piece that's been polished to look like new.

Trusting what to do with which furniture was the lesson of this time. Aero was eclectic by choice, but those disparate pieces were unified in a world of pointedly subtle, rich layers. My job, then and now, was to look at things anew, and, with a little bit of industry and magic, make something more out of what is really ordinary.

This fireplace image is from one of my earliest residential projects. I was first introduced to Alan and Gloria Siegel at an Aero party; they are longtime family friends of Laura Resen and her parents. Both are highly creative, engaging New Yorkers, and Alan is a respected collector of classic photography. Not long after, the Siegels asked me to have a look at their apartment, in one of the iconic 1930s buildings on Central Park West. The wonderful black-and-white photography was paired with somewhat severe furnishings. The space seemed very sober as a backdrop for their art.

I thought the apartment needed softening; it wanted some of its history back. One of the first important design challenges was to create and fabricate a new, classically detailed limestone mantelpiece. I paired it with a very special nineteenth-century Sultanabad carpet that had unique warm tones and beautiful botanical drawing. The coffee table was made from a pair of narrow, antique Chinese doors set in taupe lacquered frames. Other antique pieces came from the store, like the pair of old bronze stirrups that were refashioned as uplight sconces. I found the vintage photograph of the old Hayden Planetarium at the Museum of Natural History. The image is quintessentially Aero, but it is equally linked to this location. If you could look through the fireplace wall, back through the century, this is the view of the planetarium you would have seen from this apartment.

With interiors, I am always working to curate a group of special pieces—some acquired, some from Aero, some designed and custom made—that extend the interests of my clients but are also authentic to their surroundings. I love to create collections with and for people.

A view into Aero as it was beginning to fill out with more furnishings—nineteenth century and earlier antiques meeting the spirit of a midcentury aesthetic. I'd brought home the Georgian camelback club chair from London and I loved how it paired with this Paul Frankl, Chinese-modern, white cork-topped table from the 1940s. Later this special, very English chair became the model for a new set of chairs that we had made for a classic New York restaurant named Patroon.

Another important development seen in these pictures is the collection of sculpted furniture and lighting pieces, in bronze or plaster, by French artist Philippe Anthonioz. Aero was one of the first places in New York to represent this work. There was an elaborate opening party to introduce him, our version of the Soho art gallery openings of those days.

In the early years the parties and openings were many. I still have this first leather-bound Hermès guest book that was in the store. It's something to read through now, with all of its wonderfully charming entries and cast of characters.

This is the first pair of the original Aero club chairs that we made in collaboration with Jonas Upholstery. They make me think of an enormously deep, low-slung 1930s chair by Paul Frankl, whose furniture played the dramatic new urban scale. But quite often with vintage shapes I will add a slight bow to the front, a taper to the leg, or make the seat pitch back just a little more. That gentle bow is the thing that can soften upholstery a great deal. I'm not sure we ever produced more than a dozen of the chairs, as they were quite expensive and so huge, though I remember we did make one as a loveseat for a client. It turned out as big as any normal-sized sofa, and even deeper—vintage luxury brought forward.

The cobalt glass lamp on the side table is another very early Aero design. The look of rich blue cobalt was a recurring Art Deco idea in various pieces we were making, like the accent of blue silk pillows on the pale parchment-colored linen weave of the chairs.

In these early years the store added more of the types of fine decorative antiques and accessories that I was and still am interested in. It wasn't unusual for me to bring in a set of French porcelain or vintage Deco silverware, Japanese teacups or a 1970s mod lamp, to coexist with newer artisan homewares. In particular, Aero has always made new gilded pieces alongside whatever antique gilding I find, from boxes to art pieces to lamps. We also do quite a bit of gilding and lacquer work on refurbished vintage furniture. This is about finish and color as ideas that I will buy to in creating a collection. Soft lemon yellow lacquer, ivory, silver, and gold constitute the pale, soigné, 1920s palette that I was drawn to at this point in the creation of the store.

French porcelain, Indian silver, Japanese cedar, Murano glass

Silk and bronze reflected in white lacquer

I am fond of gesso and plaster on furniture, especially in the way a soft, white finish can relax both severe and elaborate shapes. This Rococo Revival mirror wasn't a major piece in itself; but when it was gessoed, the relief and carving became something different and more tactile, more of a modern silhouette. I was interested in light materials liked waxed gesso, gilding, lacquer, parchment, and cerusing, used for their luxury and handicraft in early modern design. I've always preferred the softer nature of vintage modern pieces, which have this type of light-bearing detail or patina in what they are made of.

Overleaf. One idea that drives me is to use modern things in charming, not-so-serious ways. I had just enough of one 1930s chenille-dot drapery panel to reupholster this nineteenth-century recamier.

I bought this midcentury Vladimir Kagan sectional sofa and its matching chaise from a picker on the street in front of the store, and upholstered them both in a soft linen weave. These were very tricky ones to get up the stairs for their size, and they stayed at Aero for a long time in this front corner of the loft. Sculptural as they were, in some ways no one knew what to make of them at first, but now Kagan has become quite popular again among modern collectors. The 1930s table and chairs are by Eugene Schoen. I refurbished the set in custard yellow lacquer and cream upholstery with mahogany detailing, to suggest a more luxuriant, French mood than the original, dark, American finishes of the period. The 1930s PEL umbrella stand is English, and an absolute favorite for its slightly different, chic Anglo take on tubular steel furniture.

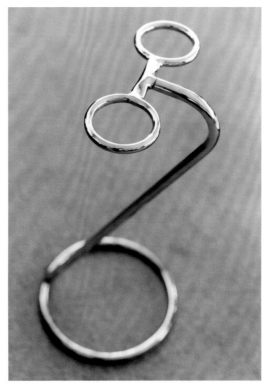

The special, tall, paneled screens with the inset windows were part of Aero's original store design. Besides the wall color and the drapery, the store was really an incredibly plain open space, and the screens became the architectural backdrop to different settings. We would move them around, sometimes together, sometimes split up, but they always had to be tied back and secured to prevent them from falling over. They were so big that they had to be hoisted in through the windows to get into the gallery. Important as they were, these screens are one thing that I brought from the old store to the new one when we moved to our current space on Broome Street.

Aero was associated with a particular group of up-and-coming artists and restorers in the early days. I met Nancy Lorenz through my Cooper Union friend Jane Henry. Both Jane and then Nancy were gilders for the store, first on refurbishing projects but soon on all kinds of pieces. We showed Nancy's beautiful gold and silver-leafed paintings for many years, as well as other works like the installation of stylized ears in *For Better Hearing,* made of gessoed plywood.

I was very taken with the idea of paleness as a way to be modern, in the spirit of Syrie Maugham and also the 1920s French modernism that was beginning to be a focus in the way we refinished vintage furniture. Also, I have always found it refreshing to live in the city with lighter colors. One example would be this 1920s Chinoiserie mahogany sideboard that I lacquered in a gentle, pretty custard yellow. The pale lacquer highlights the form and makes the fretwork detailing much more visible than it would have been in dark wood. That reversal of light and dark is an idea that I consistently turn to.

Positioned against the luminous drapery, there is a feeling of softness and refinement that is very much what the store was in this time—elegant and light.

While much of the furniture at Aero is completely refinished and reinvented, I am also drawn to vintage pieces and modern antiques of the twentieth century that can be left in their original state. The nineteenth-century mahogany chest of drawers, with its subtle bow-front and fine oval handles, was such a balanced form that it needed no reinvention. The same is true for the graceful, later midcentury nesting tables, left in their original finish. This mix, of refinished antiques, traditional furniture, and pure vintage modern furniture, was still uncommon in those days among the design showrooms and antique dealers in New York.

This picture of the gallery is a souvenir not only for the moment that it illustrates but also for the quality of the grainy film. We certainly didn't think we were documenting the store for any outside audience, so many photos of this time are simply like Polaroids, taken to remind of a certain set-up or idea that we were creating in an installation. I had started hanging art in a vintage gallery style—photographs mixed with a painting or two, some better pieces alongside found, antique images that I would frame and formalize. With this group I remember liking that the blue tones in some of the pictures softened the rest of the black-and-white photography. Any type of theme, tone, subject matter, or quality can become the throughline that makes a collection intriguing. It's always important to me to encourage clients to take that leap into art, by introducing different artists and genres that they might be interested in collecting.

This 1940s carved and partially cerused geometric lamp was a favorite for its modernism and its craft. I added a square shade in chocolate-tone paper that I liked and used a lot in those days. There is something decorative of the 1970s, in the warm reddish-browns of the wood and the paper shade, that is completely sympathetic with the boxy forms of the 1930s and '40s.

CHAPTER 6

INSIDE OUTSIDE

MY APARTMENT, DOWNSTAIRS

Several years after I opened Aero, an opportunity came up to move into a new apartment in my building on Sixtieth Street. It was on the third floor, which was nice in that I wouldn't have to walk up quite as many flights of stairs every day.

But most of all, most magically, this third-story apartment had a large terrace in the back. The outdoor space was literally bigger than the apartment itself, with a skylight in the middle of the roof deck of the antique store downstairs.

Some row houses with shop fronts from the turn of the century were structured this way—the buildings would step back on the first or second level to create breezeways and clearance from the houses on the facing street. This formed a backyard of sorts, especially if you were on the right floor to use the courtyard, or that piece of the extending lower roof as a terrace.

Having an outdoor space in the city was the beginning of something very important for me. I loved my urbanized version of a traditional back door, peeking out onto something green. Ever since then, in New York, I have had a terrace garden and a door to outside.

The most striking element of the inside of this apartment was its white-stained parquet floors. They reminded me of my first days of going to the New York art galleries uptown. I was always especially taken with the light-stained or pickled floors like those at the Robert Miller Gallery on Fifty-Seventh Street. So, after the dark floors at Aero with all the pale drapery, this new space gave me an opportunity to do the reverse—paint the walls a rich, deep color against white floors. It was the first time I used them, but light floors in this simple, modern, gallery mood have become a recurring design element for me ever since, in my own homes and in a good number of residences that I've designed.

There was also the question of my furniture and how it fit the new equation of this apartment. Just as I was buying modern antiques and rejuvenating them for Aero and for clients—taking dark things and making them light, for example—at home I was collecting American antiques, but leaving them warm and wooded against the dark walls. Combinations of antique wood, burnt-orange porcelain, amber and deep-cobalt glass, all suggest a more traditional attitude with dark walls. By comparison, my upstairs apartment had been light

and airy and casual, and much more designed in certain ways, with the tailored character of the leather, palomino, tortoise, and sisal and just the worn, soft colors of my antique Persian rug. Likewise my house in the country had a rich, dark bedroom with a light living room. Here, I inverted all that.

I doubt I'd ever imagined placing American antiques against the setting of a light floor, or having a back door in New York. But bringing my love of old and American things and the outdoors into a new apartment allowed me to switch ideas around. The setting changes to make those traditional items more graphic, chic, and modern. This is what I sometimes call traditional modern design. Accordingly, when I've been asked about design and where certain ideas come from over the years, I often explain that for me design is a series of loops, with each focus, each detail or revision, leading to the next one. What I mean is that one decision always prompts another. This apartment is the product of previous spaces, and here I developed things I liked and discarded others on the way to my next apartment, on Fifty-Seventh Street. Later on, this place again became a touchstone, and some of the ways I was living here made a comeback in how I live and what I design today.

We all evolve in the way we live, and especially in the confidence to know what we like and who we are. There is always context, always something we react to in the surrounding neighborhood of ideas. A choice to continue in the same direction, refine and simplify, or go an entirely different way.

This apartment with its many collections was a reaction to the more polished modern world that was evolving at the store. The dark walls come out of Aero, but the furnishings and the richer palette are a return to the comfort of the world of antiques that I have always enjoyed living with.

The Victorian mahogany hat stand, with its classical baldacchino turning, is one piece that you might have expected to see in a shop of fine Irish and English antiques, more than at Aero. It originally came into the store from a pair of talented antique pickers and New York characters, my friends Robert Loughlin and Gary Carlson. Many people wanted to buy it right away. I really probably needed to sell it but instead I saved it in my office and eventually brought it home. Merging nineteenth- and twentieth-century ideals, with all their contradictions and also their affinities, is what interested me then and still does now. I find it charming, too, that this photo was taken while the 1956 film version of *Moby Dick* played on the TV, adding to the juxtaposition of eras in this moment.

The main furniture and all my tiger and leopard velvet pillows are reunited at home after their long jobs as placeholders for other things to come at Aero. The mood is different, though, with the deep sage green walls and the heavy drapery made of a silvery green woven plaid. The curtain rod spans the wall again, but here the drapes are lined in felt to block out the light. There is sometimes power in a darker room, a kind of cocooned comfort. I was experimenting here with something richer, and even though light rooms are prevalent in my interiors, I also like and often do dark rooms in the spirit of an English library or den.

The colors in this space—green, bronze, and wood—were a direct response to living with a garden on my terrace. The world of the garden has been a throughline from childhood to my country houses to my city life. It's what feels like home to me, and now garden design is a major and very satisfying part of the work I do. Gardening has a wonderful decency, and is such a fundamental aspect of classic twentieth-century interior decoration. In this apartment, all of these notes would sound in a very traditional key but for the white floor, which keeps everything modern and offbeat.

This apartment includes a number of very sentimental objects that belonged to my mentor and former boss at Polo, Jeff Walker. Working for Jeff inspired me on many levels, from the kinds of antiques I was buying to the strong presence of fashion and tailoring as part of my style. He was an enormously talented, driven, commanding man, and personally he was very dapper in the classic Ralph Lauren menswear tradition. But another aspect of Jeff was that he was from California, and a West Coast informality showed through in his tastes. His office at Polo was modern and white with a pool-blue painted-concrete floor. Continental antiques lived next to American rustic objects. This vintage Wolf suit form stood in one corner, dressed in a red-white-and-blue Fourth of July folk-art outfit. I keep both out at my country house now, though at first in this apartment I used the suit form as a kind of pinboard for images. On the other side of the armoire is a large standing basket that Jeff gave to me at one point when he was redecorating his apartment. I still use it as my hamper. It makes me think of the beachy, easy element, the sisal and canvas that Jeff brought east and mixed into his New York life. I learned from that mix, and over time recognized what my own source of casual and simple was, in the American country antiques of my childhood.

I bought the 1920s armoire on an antiquing trip upstate, and used it here as the primary closet for my shirts and suits. I love the plain, raised panel of the doors and the dark, dry, matte finish on the wood, cracked and crazed with age. I still use the armoire as a coat closet in the living room of my apartment on Fifty-Seventh Street. The small nineteenth-century Italian landscape painting above it is probably the first proper antique painting I ever bought. Most certainly it was something I saw in a different light following my trips to art galleries in London and Paris with Jeff and Ralph.

My desk was a group of patinated, timeworn, odd and broken things that I kept as they were and didn't choose to send off to be refinished, like the increasing flow of antiques that we were refurbishing in the store and for clients. I found the 1840s slant-front desk on another shopping trip upstate, and used it next to the sofa as both a side and writing table. The leather blotter is worn to the point of almost disappearing. I loved it that way and wouldn't have replaced it. The same is true for the vintage photo of a chorale frieze on a cathedral. The disintegrating emulsion on the paper becomes part of the image, while the handsome nineteenth-century profile of the frame was its own reason for buying the piece: oftentimes I will buy artwork just for an old frame. The chair here was one of three crumbling, early Chippendale-style chairs that I'd found at a favorite antique store in the city, and the only usable one of the set that had most of its back intact. I saved all the broken fragments together in a box for many years, and used the other ruined chairs at Aero in displays. Later I did have them carefully restored and subsequently used them as the model for a classical chair in my first furniture collection.

The crystal inkwell was Jeff Walker's, from his desk at Polo. The brass and bronze English lamp is made from an antique coffee urn. This piece has moved back and forth between home and Aero at different times over the years.

The plate is one of several beautiful pieces of Imari porcelain and stoneware in the apartment. This one is Copeland Imari from 1860. There was a wonderful china shop on Greenwich Avenue right in the heart of the West Village that was one of my constant haunts. Sadly, places like this barely exist anymore; but there I would pick up early Wedgwood dishes, antique silver and crystal, and the varieties of individual platters and other serving pieces that I have been collecting ever since. I was making investments in these special pieces early on, even when I knew I couldn't really afford them. Years later, I now turn to their intricate designs in the making of new patternwork for carpets and textiles.

With the earthy greens in the rest of the apartment, the bedroom didn't want to be white; it needed to be rich, too. I painted it a khaki that was almost the color of Dijon mustard. Khaki is a tricky tone that can easily become flat and beige. I usually like it in fabric more than in paint. But, every once in a while, I'll see a stony, richer khaki in a vintage interior that can be quite beautiful and interesting. So when I use khaki, I like it to feel vintage and colorful.

The bedroom walls have a gallery-style hanging of many types of art, as I'd begun to present artwork at Aero. One piece here that was tacked to the wall, not yet framed, is the large, inky blue, 1940s Rand McNally star chart. I'd recently bought it upstate, as I recall, for just $75; I held on to its sale tag for the longest time. I've always kept the star chart near my bed, like a piece of the night sky, and it has become one of my talismans through the years. I also love seeing the early studio portrait here in its oval mat, one of a pair dating to 1915 that I'd found in their original frames and glass. On this one the glass was broken but I left it intact for as long as it would hold together.

CHAPTER 7

WARM MODERN

KIPS BAY

In 1999 I was invited to design a space in the annual Kips Bay showhouse in New York. First staged in 1973, this showhouse is the flagship fundraising event for the Kips Bay Boys & Girls Club, but it's best known as one of the premier gatherings of the year for the city's design community. It is always quite an honor to be part of this experience.

The suite I did at Kips Bay was a turning point for me and Aero. Alongside my work in interiors and the store, by the end of the 1990s I had begun to design more home furnishings, including licensed goods for companies other than my own. This showhouse was one of the first places where I used a group of these new furnishings that were just beginning to launch. It was an important and exciting public introduction for me as a product designer.

Something of a balance was crystallized in this project that became the style I was to be associated with for quite some time. This was coined by various writers and often referred to as warm modernism.

I didn't spearhead this style of warm modernism, and I haven't ever been the only one working in it, but I do think it describes something that I have always been most inclined toward in design, that maybe I was highlighting in a more deliberate way during this period. The clue is in what this warmth refers to. It's not just a sense of materiality or color. Quiet as I am personally, I tend to be warm and very domestic. I don't like cold, austere, modern interiors; I don't really gravitate to stark minimalism where all traces of daily living are hidden. So this notion of domestic and personal warmth is how I have always thought of warm modernism.

For me it's the evidence of use, of soul and origin, that make something reminiscent and warm; it is to be in the presence of the past. Even though I tend to be governed by modernism in the scale and perception of what I design, it is really the things from the barn that still pull me—the old, distressed, rustic, unassuming. Those are the details I miss if they're not there.

I have never wandered too far from the upstate boy that I was, looking for antiques that are so interesting in their wear and scars that they become sculptural and elegant in their own way. These items have always been part of my home and included in the store, at my insistence. And even during this time when I was doing more interiors, these rough pieces with great lines and character, that cost next to nothing, were the ones that I had to convince clients to let me bring into their houses.

For the Kips Bay showhouse, in a grand, formal, Gilded Age house just off Fifth Avenue on Eighty-Second Street, I was happy to have the space that no one else really wanted: the old servant's quarters on the uppermost floor, at the top of a narrow, twisting staircase. Because they were a pair of custodial rooms, they lacked the architectural flourishes of the main residential floors, but there was something quiet and modern in the plainness of the space and its wealth of natural skyward light.

I had a new line of bath furniture and fittings that I had just designed for the bath company Waterworks, so it was a logical fit to adopt the idea of a bathroom for the showhouse and stretch it into something more of a modern, spa-like suite. That was the fantasy of this project—to think about a bathroom and bath materials in an interior way. And also the reverse—to think about how to bring real furniture design into the bathroom.

This was different, too, from what I was doing downtown in the store. A bathroom is a fully fixtured, architectural space in so many ways, and this showhouse let me do some wonderful things in construction that were well beyond what I could show at Aero. I believe it was this different direction for a modern interior that stood out for many, when modernism was still perceived to be something bare and intellectual, or otherwise slick and youthful.

To furnish the space, I brought in refurbished vintage pieces from Aero along with new furniture that I was making locally in limited editions for the store. I included other pieces here and there from a group of private-label accessories for Tiffany & Co., my very first commercial product design collaboration of any kind. So this interior was not just about a downtown style, or my mix of modern and rustic antiques; it was also about presenting a viewpoint in furniture and object design that would be accessible to people beyond the rarity of that showhouse environment.

WORDS AND PICTURES

As the product-design side of my business grew, I was required to write detailed new item descriptions, Aero profiles, and design statements as part of the official communications with my partners. I knew I had to make sure that I was not just talking now but also writing in a disciplined way that was a clear translation of Aero.

So it happened that I met writer Lisa Light through Waterworks. She'd written for them about my bath line and then I invited her to write for me about the suite at Kips Bay. We quickly moved to other assignments that I thought could use some wordcraft. A new hotel I was designing. Press releases and holiday cards. More product partnerships. Newer media, a website, periodic essays. Together, we have tackled the careful work of creating a consistent voice in business and design.

Over a dozen years and more, Lisa has become my collaborator and written memory on so many of the studio's projects. Like other characters from my life in these pages, we have grown together, and she is here with me. She brings a lyricism and the ability to make writing feel visual, even when I am inclined to be plainspoken and conversational. But then, I like to tell a story, and I think there is real integrity in the rhythm and tensions of formal writing, just like the balance of differing forces in a formal design process.

Nevertheless, I've been surprised in recent years at how often I've been told not to worry about writing, since people are reading less and less about design. They tune in for the pictures, want only articles and sound bites. I have to fight for any of the writing that I do to be delivered intact in this more composed way. But there is something to be said, still, for a graciously crafted announcement, or any design text with an informative narrative and thoughtful phrasing. These are designed objects as much as a chair, a faucet, or a house. And so together with my family of collaborators, I make products; but also, I have written one and now another of these books.

In this world of tweets and blog posts and instantly updated histories, that may make me old-fashioned. But in the warmth of words to go with modern pictures, I believe in a literary tradition.

I've always found inspiration in the 1930s book *Modern Interiors* by Emily Genauer. I actually have two vintage copies: one in beige bookcloth, and this one, with its wonderful blue cover, that is my favorite. This book and then the echo of bookcloth and leather on the Aero lamp, laid down in a whitewashed Aero tray, form a very intentional scene. They are emblematic of what was incredibly interesting to me that I was studying and interpreting at this time: forms from the earlier period of modernism as they might be today. The notion of the antique modern thing. When I look at these pictures, that was the movie of this interior in my head; that I wanted to convey not just decoration but a time, a scholarship, and a history that existed in the bath plumbing I had designed, and all the other furnishings I was beginning to produce within this idea of a vintage modern aesthetic.

I had imagined this pair of attic rooms as a sitting room and bathroom ensuite. I wanted the space to be about a merging of past and present, with my brand-new, retro-antique plumbing and furniture in this serene bath retreat. It was my update of the time and place that had generated such rooms: not only the forms of the 1930s and '40s but also the glamour and intelligence of the city lifestyle. For me, the history of grand, modern, urban bath quarters, with their private dressing rooms and lounges, formed a really compelling and elegant concept to explore, more so than the later convention of a bathroom grafted onto a master bedroom.

This walnut table was positioned as a desk right as you entered the space from the stairs. It was one of a pair I had made with a set of vintage aluminum legs that I'd been saving for a new design. I brought in the vintage nautical photograph and the ebonized turned-wood pedestal from my house on Long Island. The refinished tubular chrome chair was from Aero. These pieces come from different worlds—industrial and artisanal—but they resonate together as dark punctuation in a light setting. Ebony, sable, and brown offset the pale layers of ivory, palomino, and celadon that were so appealing to me. This combination quickly filtered into the work of Aero.

For the sitting room, I wanted to extend the tile and mosaic out of the bath, in the way that a laboratory, an apothecary, or even a bank or theater lobby was clad in these materials in the heyday of the Machine Age. Those spaces were all very durable yet still materially luxurious. And plain, unpatterned marble mosaic is one of my favorite surfaces, something that is both classical and modern. I love the sparkle of it.

I imagined a tiled platform for the daybed, built in a favorite square-tile, running bond configuration with a simple stepped base and crown. This same tiling covered the walls in the bathroom area as well. The mattress-tufted cushion in a Bergamo linen weave is a type of upholstery, tailored but simple, that I like for its hand-sewn, rolled imperial edge. I'd bought the pair of Deco chairs for the refinement of their slender wood detailing, and reupholstered them in a Japanese fabric with a bit of raffia in it. For softness and sound, I chose to blanket the walls in the simplest stony celadon Bergamo sateen, using this most minimal fabric almost like a paint color. I do find that an upholstered room provides an essential muted feeling that one senses all around, in movement as much as acoustics. This was a choice here to make sure that the hard, bright sitting room did have a soft, restful quietness about it.

Adjacent to the sitting room through a large framed opening, the bathroom area was centered on a huge walnut double vanity with its new Aero faucets. I based the vanity on a similarly large laboratory table that I'd made as a cash wrap for the Aero store. I was thinking a lot in those days about work spaces and Bauhaus design, that kind of elegant, academic utility from the early twentieth century. Other details gave the washstand more luxury—the carved, stepped profile of the marble top, the nickel-plated cap feet that came directly out of a 1930s world. The metalwork was echoed in the plumbing and the classic industrial-style box lights that I had hand-made in nickel. Helping me to fabricate these pieces and construct this environment was my Cooper Union friend and master builder, Randy Polumbo. Randy is a meticulous contractor as well as an accomplished artist and sculptor.

Across from the vanity we built an oversized niche of wide, thick glass shelves into the tile. The idea here was to magnify the scale of the niche and the glass as though this were a magically exploded medicine chest with no doors on it. Everything about this bathroom—the vanity, the shelves, the shower—had that exaggeration of scale. At the same time, it was all-important that every detail be gently crafted so that the space remained soft and reflective, not loud.

This showhouse for me is also a document of the first generation of my product designs. I think of the world of old New York that inspired much of this work; how preserving or re-creating the romance of that era of the city is what I wanted Aero to be about. It is what I was studying, when most of the serious vintage modern antiques in shops around town were still Continental and English. The rediscovery of the very fine, American midcentury object was still fairly new.

The modular "skyscraper" cabinets were from my original Waterworks collection. For this item I liked the idea of a walnut cabinet that had drawers in different sizes and configurations, like a puzzle. The form owes a debt to the designer Paul Frankl, who was working in the optimism of the skyscraper age, with a perspective that was bold and architectural, truly of New York. Very few of these cabinets were made but they were a great, shallow size for storage in small spaces even beyond the bathroom.

The tapered cigar floor lamp and the turned candlestick lamp in raw oak are both early Aero lighting designs. The latter was based on a pair of tall polished-mahogany candlesticks from a church. I had begun experimenting with the freshness of raw oak and raw walnut in the lamps and upholstery frames we had made for the store, as a way to make traditional woodwork feel modern. The round gessoed and gilded mirror, like the mirrors above the bathroom vanity, were all made for Aero by Gill & Lagodich, my favorite antiquarian framers in New York. I still partner with them today on all of my archival framing. And the glass vase on the antique ceramic pedestal was one of the prototypes for Tiffany, from my first product collection outside of Aero.

At the shallow end of the bathroom, I built in a six-by-ten wall-to-wall shower with a tiled bench and a deep window ledge. The materials are so basic, with ivory tile and canvas curtains—even terrycloth upholstery on the nearby chrome bench—but the craft is complete in a very lavish way. The mosaic floor extends into the shower basin; the tile envelops the entire space. The Aero fittings, with showerheads and spraybars jetting in from the facing walls, are plated in warm, silvery nickel. Waterworks was one of the first companies to start importing classic English plumbing to the United States, but this collection of mine was intentionally more industrial and American, with stepped profiles inspired by telescopes and other Machine Age instruments.

The amplified scale of this shower is by its nature a custom project. Here it was a fun thing to invent as an advertisement for what was possible on a luxury level; but the idea is also adaptable and practical. From this concept, there are times now when I do forgo a traditional tub in a small bathroom in favor of one larger shower.

CHAPTER 8

LOFT MATERIALS

HISTORICAL NEW YORK

From the late 1990s through the first years of the 2000s, a new real estate boom in loft-rich lower Manhattan brought a fresh wave of residents to Soho and Tribeca. With their arrival came more designers and architects who specialized in the iconic loft conversions of the day—very urban, modern, and materially minimal. Lofts up to that point were mostly refined versions of the original industrial spaces artists had first co-opted in the previous decades, with exposed columns, brick walls, and the raw elegance of a vast open room to define this new living style.

But there was also an invitation to go further, to rethink and retrofit a loft space at another level. Lofts could be homes with every amenity, invested with much more architectural detail and classical craftsmanship, yet be faithful to their urban history. And this development merged with my interests and studies as well.

Around this time I took a personal step forward and bought the apartment in the city that I still live in today. This apartment is in a classic 1930s building on Fifty-Seventh Street, with

a vintage New York formality. The space has giant floor-to-ceiling casement windows and otherwise simple architecture that has the suggestion of an artist's loft, like a nineteenth-century painter's studio. The renovation of that apartment was a full leap into the design ideas I introduced at the Kips Bay showhouse. I look at this space in depth in my first book, *American Modern*.

Certain clients came to Aero because they had seen the Fifty-Seventh Street apartment published in several magazine stories, or knew about my work at Kips Bay. Some of these clients were Soho émigrés looking to move into lofts, and the homes that I designed for them covered a considerable stylistic and domestic range. On one end of the spectrum, I think of the more feminine and European residence I designed on two floors of a new loft building, with the room sense of an earlier townhouse and a layout for a young family. On the other, there is the masculine, classic, old New York loft that I am including here. This was a sleek and even sexy place, full of harder edges, lavish collections, and pure social spaces that I designed for a modern New York businessman-bachelor.

What I have here is a series of snapshots I took of this loft in the fall of 2002, as it was being completed. These pictures aren't so much about seeing the whole interior as they are a look into the quite tailored details of construction and materiality that can drive the kind of design I am talking about. In this particular case the details came out of an intensive historical restoration

that allowed an old building to recover some of its authenticity and soul.

Not all lofts are created equal, and this one had an unusually august pedigree. The location was a penthouse floor in the American Thread Building, just across Canal Street in Tribeca. Built in 1896 in grand Renaissance Revival style, the space had never been a factory or warehouse; rather, it was situated at the top of the city's old Wool Exchange and once held a formal boardroom and a series of mercantile clubs. The loft was centered around a beautifully paneled rotunda with a large oculus of stained glass.

These nineteenth-century features survived in the core of the space. But the whole perimeter of the loft—the former offices and clubs—had been robbed of almost all the original detail during an early 1980s loft conversion. It suffered from horrible, dropped eight-foot ceilings and other mediocrities, and the bathrooms and kitchen that had been put in lacked all character to match the soaring luxury of the main spaces.

The project depended on vintage architectural craft to re-create those rooms with the enormous height and light and also the elegance of the original interior. And it's often the case that kitchens and bathrooms require the most deliberate reinvention of cabinetry, metalwork, finishes, and fixturing when undergoing a renovation, if only to equal what remains of the fine workmanship in an older building. This is especially true of the kitchens I like to design, to be historically resonant but also functional and new. In this way, the new construction here, with its antique modern associations, became the bridge to the exquisitely crafted, architectural, early modern furniture that was then collected for the home.

This space was ultimately about reconfiguring a true remnant of grand old New York as a classically expansive, refined apartment. It is the meshing of two eras and two personas, each peculiar to the city: the industrial-era clubroom businessman of this building's past, and the modern Tech Age investor who would move here in the twenty-first century.

And this renovation played out in a way that is also true of so many projects I work on. The modern devotee discovers traditional tastes, while the traditional client craves the modern. Though this client started out with an image of creating a modern loft, he ultimately gravitated to a space with more historical graces. My job was to make the marriage of the two, bringing back sumptuous materials and encouraging conservancy, but also letting the apartment be experienced in a bolder, less embellished, easy, modern way.

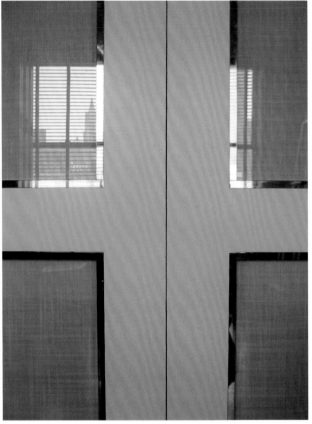

Every door, cabinet, piece of millwork and hardware that we added to the loft was designed so that nothing would stand out as too new or invasive. The point was to take classic materials—mahogany, nickel, marble—and apply them to a new pared-down set of forms, though still as individually crafted as in a much older estate. This approach helped to link the surviving nineteenth-century architecture to the early twentieth-century modern direction that was right for the client.

The huge scale of the space also demanded design solutions with grand proportions and height. For the corner kitchen, I created a cage of partition walls with tall, slender folding doors and a system of transom windows that reached the ceiling. Linen is sandwiched between panes of glass in each door to create a screened enclosure, but its semi-translucence still allows the city's skyline views and light from the windows to be seen through the interior glass. Each door panel is articulated in a nickel frame for more shimmer and definition: new details that steer the constructed shell toward Deco-modern style.

The entryway walls are covered in panels of parchment-colored, varnished linen. To me they recall vintage varnished linen luggage, both luxurious and fresh. The angular Zig Zag chair by Gerrit Rietveld is a 1934 design. This is one of the first significant auction pieces that I purchased as I began building a collection of modernist furniture for the client.

In the rotunda we restored the beautiful mosaic floor and all the original oak paneling. The all-important anteroom, which was to be a bar, demanded a strong set of surfaces that would be equally intriguing. Dark wood and sleek, heavy folding doors set a tone, along with this patterned and grooved, cast-steel floor tile that I had found, which had come out of a nineteenth-century factory. The juxtaposition was dramatic, and I had to convince the client to use it, but the floor evokes some of the world of the machine that I wanted to capture, from that era when industrial components were still crafted to be visually handsome, if not even decorative. To me, metalwork is such a vital dimension of the world of the modern, and this highly striking element drives attention to many other smaller details of intricate Machine Age metal hardware that filter through the reconstruction.

This mahogany and brass Adolf Loos daybed from the early 1920s is one of the most important antiques in the loft, and exceptionally unique. Loos was primarily an architect, so there aren't very many examples of his furniture to be found, and I haven't ever come across anything quite like this piece again. When I think of a Loos interior, it has all of the same extremely refined, seductive, dark qualities. I think of paneled rooms in simple but rich woods, elaborate marbles, and brass and bronze as much as white metals like nickel—the earliest moment of Viennese modernism, different than its French or American counterparts. Dark and elegant libraries, men's clubs, and even banks of the era share this pared-down, masculine aesthetic, and that is the spirit that governed how this loft was furnished.

The daybed was paired with a billiard table in a section of the main living space. I wanted it to feel like seating in a vintage executive office, more tailored than a bed. To match the richness of the antique, the upholstery needed the intensity of a deep color rather than a neutral. We did a hand-stitched mattress-tufted cushion and loose pillows in a mossy, almost silver-green cotton velvet, along with contrasting pillows in an ultra-dark aubergine velvet that picked up the tones of the wood—both more "colorful" colors that came out of the world of furniture at Aero.

The guest bedroom occupied one end of the arc of the loft. A room was created with tall pocket doors that opened onto the living space, so that this chamber could become a part of the public area when not in use. For this reason the furnishings needed to feel more social and lounge-like, and less of the bedroom. I designed the saddle-stitched leather platform to hold a mattress like a giant chaise, framed by a high, asymmetrical, felted corner screen of the kind you might see in the interiors of Jean-Michel Frank. The chocolate cashmere throw trimmed in kid leather was from Aero. This is a palette of luxe materials that have enormous style even when they are very simple and understated. Dark shades of sable, taupe, and cocoa, and lighter ones of palomino, fawn, and smoky grey, are all of a vintage modern moment but also, in a more sensuous way, seem to me like the rich, natural colors of animal fur.

I designed the raw teak bench, below, as a modern interpretation of a more antique piece of furniture. The carving is not just square, but beveled and softened with slight curves that bring to mind a classical stone bench. I upholstered it in the same all-silk carpet that was used on the floor of the bedrooms: a beguiling and precious material that is more widely seen now but was very new to Aero at the time.

More than any other place in the loft, the mammoth marbled master bath is infused with an American, Radio City–like glamour. As with the kitchen, this was a newly constructed space that had to stand up to the grandeur of the loft's original Beaux Arts architecture. Black-and-white marble establish an urban, retro, graphic feeling, with gleaming strips of nickel trim paneling the huge slabs from floor to ceiling. Black or other dark marbles are often the sort of thing to be expected in a rich and refined powder room, but I liked this marble's masculine character for the counters, floor, and tub deck instead of a more predictable, classic white. The Aero faucet, also in nickel, features a signature three-part propeller handle, while most traditional valves have four-part handles. The very special nickel framework of the gigantic medicine chest is translated into the frame of the nickel-plated vanity below, with its plain white painted doors. The modern-era simplicity of these doors relates in an essential way to the glass-stop framework of the panelized, folding kitchen doors. And just as there is linen sandwiched between the glass in the kitchen doors, there is silk paired to mirror and nickel in the structured and ribbed Roman shade of the bathroom. I think of its form here almost like a vintage modern lampshade.

CHAPTER 9

ANTIQUE STORE

AERO LIGHT AND DARK

I know it is ironic that the most constant idea in my design life is duality. I speak of it often, and probably the notion of duality and contradiction is hardwired into my Gemini nature. I like the balance that comes from reconciling opposites. I instinctively turn one way when I might be expected to go another. I have always been drawn to the fluctuating rhythms that make unexpected pairs and partners more unique and interesting.

Aero has been full of these balances—the traditional and modern, of course, but also casual and elegant, masculine and feminine, zig and zag—in differing combinations over the years. This certainly has always been true of the colors I've liked and chosen in my work. I tend to use colors that are rich but neutral, though I've also gravitated to bolder contrasts of light and dark in different periods of time. This set of pictures is about one of those periods in the store, in the early 2000s, around the same time as the interiors in the preceding chapters.

At home and in several of the residences I was designing, I was turning to a pale surrounding, with light floors, silvery metalwork, soft twilight colors and luster.

In the store, with its increasing layers of furniture and decoration, something more of a counterpoint occurred: the silhouettes of light furniture, upholstery, and objects held in a darker room. And from there, I began more two-tone experiments in a lot of the vintage furniture I was refinishing, with soft, fair, natural materials against a darker sculptural frame. The catalyst of this change is simple. At a certain point I took up the three carpets at Aero, leaving the ebonized floors bare to make much more of a direct impact, dark and shiny as can be. This was, in practical ways, simply a choice to emphasize a rich design feature that was already there. It felt logical to look at the space with the carpets up, to contrast the idea of light floors in one area of my life with dark ones in another. And even though I hadn't done a thing to them, the floors started to get noticed and were favorites with many clients of that time.

As part of this shift, I started to use purer white finishes and brighter, whiter fabrics. I had already been lightening, cerusing, and whitewashing wood furniture in my own vintage way, leaving the grain showing but looking more elegant and crafted. This look was not farmhouse white, English white, or minimalist opaque white, but soft, antique modernist white.

And I do think light finishes are refreshing. I see in them the relaxed look of California Modern design, in the midcentury, Hollywood work of designers like Samuel Marx, and much later, John Dickinson, too. To me they feel essential, refined, and interesting.

But in those days when dark, lacquered, and polished furniture were favorites, these new white and off-white finishes were different and a surprise. Any number of pieces I handled this way often stayed on the floor for a long time and were more difficult to sell. Now they look chic and they're very popular. It's one of the measures of the time that's passed to recall how new and startling this particular contrast of light and dark once was in the store.

MAKING MEMOS

With all this refurbished vintage furniture to be shared, I think another intriguing dimension of Aero is how we provide information on our pieces to other designers. After all, I shop for antiques and other furniture for my own clients, so I try to serve my design colleagues here with the kind of materials I would expect to receive myself.

I began my career at a time when antique dealers to the trade produced individual memos on each piece in their store, and every designer used these memos to present prospective purchases to their clients. This is really a classic part of the etiquette of design, to provide pictures of an item along with a detailed description—its measurements, history, materials, and price—all nicely formatted on a good sheet of stationery. We have always created such memos at Aero to share product information in this customary way. To me it's an emblem of a certain kind of gracious tradition that makes this store special.

I can remember in my early days, going around Kings Road and Pimlico Road in London, or the antique stores uptown in New York, and collecting memos on various pieces. Some places would have folio books or a card catalog with photocopies of their stock; other times a dealer would take a Polaroid of the inquired-about item or allow you to take a Polaroid. The memos could run from the most beautiful, formal documents for serious acquisitions, with fine photographs and written sheets in their own folders, to the simpler clipping of a snapshot to a printout. At Aero, as all these pictures indicate, we posed some things more formally and others far more momentarily and casually.

Memos are a designer's tool and they are still a necessity. It is the designer's job to interpret a request and extrapolate options in a creative, sophisticated, advisory way—not just to source items and compile tear sheets. One can't expect a client to respond to special and often costly items without proper documentation in a well-designed presentation. And as a shopkeeper I see how it can be equally punishing to leave a customer in the store guessing about a product's background or the historical context for a price.

Sadly, I find today that when I am shopping for my clients, the traditional memo is much changed. Many boutiques and dealers send their information ad-hoc, often by email, with little graphic organization, no formatting or formal letterhead. We in the design studio have to remake our own memos for these goods in order to present them properly to clients. It is also true that as more customers shop for themselves, digital photography and smart phones allow anyone to snap a picture in a store at any time; and research can be done online without ever having to go into a store at all to talk to someone knowledgeable. The art of a certain kind of personal transaction in design really is disappearing.

But that is all the more reason to keep doing what we do at Aero. Providing documentation is but one of the parts of discovering something wonderful, of coming into a store, trusting the preparation, choices and service behind a piece for sale; of interacting with other people in the trail of an object.

And so these pictures. They were never intended to be put together as a group, these images of all kinds of chairs and tables, lamps and furniture that are the by-product of making memos. But in retrospect they tell a story about the kind of place Aero is. I liked the idea of seeing some of them assembled, each part of a greater sum accrued over many years, almost every one of these pieces now sold and gone.

Some of these items were illustrious; many others passed through these doors with no great fanfare. I bought and sold them all because I thought they were beautiful and well designed. Their provenance is that they come from Aero, and will hopefully be remembered that way over time.

The store is always incrementally evolving as pieces sell and are replaced. But sometimes a complete shift is useful to bring familiar things into a new focus. At one point I took the carpets up and left the dark floors bare. This picture captures the moment when the glamour of the silk drapes with the high-gloss floor was so evident. The pale furniture looks bolder and yet somehow quite classical against the rich, ebonized wood. I pay attention to light and dark all the time, but here, there is also the added ingredient of what is dark and polished versus some of the softer, more antique finishes that I gravitate to.

In the world of antiques of all types, there are always more chairs to be found than anything else. Tables and beds tend to be taken apart. Coffee tables are a relatively new invention. But chairs go in every room. We have had no lack of chairs come through the store, and I have far too many special ones that I keep in storage.

Starting with chairs, many of the furniture pictures in this and subsequent chapters come from the stockpiles of memo photos that have been saved at the studio and store. Some I took for inspiration as I was beginning to create my own furniture collections; others became the starting point, in a detail or shape, for what to do in a room design. On this page are two variations on an Aero ivory chair. They're extremely different in what they emphasize, but much the same in terms of how I think about tailoring, silhouette, and finish. The painted Rococo chair was one of those antiques that I wanted to keep in the state I found it, with its soft, chipped, patinated color. The 1940s Chinese Modern chair was given new ivory silk upholstery in the spirit of a formal dining chair, with a darker finish on the frame. This piece later became the model for a dining chair in my furniture collection.

Around this time, we introduced a group of furniture by Australian designer Sam Whiteman, who wasn't much known yet in the United States. His pieces had a whimsical, decorative inventiveness and a wavelike sculpture to them, primarily in white papier-mâché and plaster, and some in black. They have always reminded me of the modernist white parchment furniture of Samuel Marx. Decorative in a different way are the classic, lacquered, antique Chinese chest and table in a nearby corner. Traditional Chinese design contains many such essential forms that have been continually interpreted, not only in Chinese Modern furniture of the 1940s, but also in the choices and work of designers throughout the twentieth century.

This is a snapshot taken just after I'd done a reset of the floor, with the carpets set back down. The palette is softer again, reinvented in a different light and dark way with pale tones of palomino, parchment, and calfskin against warm, woody teak and walnut, and oxblood leather. This is a color range I often return to that has a more casual, California Modern air than the formality of ebony and ivory. And these tones worked with the slightly later style of these pieces of midcentury furniture that I had found and recovered at this point to put in the store, in the fun of creating a new stage set. The screen is a piece I designed, made of whitewashed maple with beveled mirror. The 1950s Italian sofa and chairs are upholstered in nubuck leather. A Gibbings chair is covered in raffia.

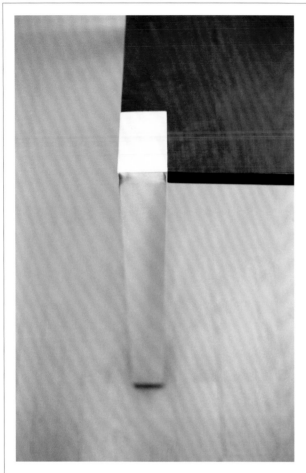

Some classic Aero designs in metal, wood, and upholstery.
Many of the things that I make are simple, streamlined,
and square edged, but crafted in fine materials that I always
return to. A soft, polished aluminum leg paired with a
waxed walnut tabletop. The vintage 1930s form of the first-
generation Geneva armchair, in enigmatic, silvery velvet.
A Parsons-like cerused-oak Keith side table with an inset,
thick Lucite top, first made as stacking shelving units for the
Aero shop annex downstairs.

I do really love large coffee tables and think of them as so modern. This was an unusual, classically detailed one from the 1920s, made of rich, mahogany-toned lacquered panels from a nineteenth-century Japanese screen. The store client who purchased it chose this table for a new country house that she was furnishing. She is a special one who has a creative, artistic, quite bold and modern point of view in her art and style, while favoring more traditional interiors. We finally met later on, when she began the project of a wonderful duplex apartment in New York, and we have worked together ever since. She is certainly my friend, and now we are back at that first country house, adding some different new and old things.

Silhouettes of decades, refurbished in glove leather and calfskin. Fine garment leathers sourced from the fashion world have long been favorites of mine for modern upholstery. An original 1930s burled-wood Deco side chair; we made a very few special, custom commissions of this piece with Jonas Upholstery. A 1950s California Modern steel rod table base, found and refashioned with a new crafted top of saddle-stitched leather. A pair of 1940s Gibbings armchairs reupholstered in spotted calfskin. I like this particular color of the calfskin and use it often on vintage tubular chrome chairs. But with a soft, light mahogany frame, almost equal in tone, the wood and leather are particularly beautiful together.

In the store, the odd mixture of art that can occur is very much in the spirit of a classic, older nineteenth-century gallery. This particular grouping was inspired by the shared colors and graphic qualities of the Picasso throw on the sofa and the charming, naive 1940s painting of the girl with a giant blue-green bottle. The uniqueness of the collection came from these found and somewhat mysterious pieces that lived in the store like old friends. The girl is one who stayed here for a long while, and in retrospect, her portrait is a thing that I am still most curious about. I wonder where she is now.

A spring day in the store. The flow of burlwood on a cabinet, the curves of a yin and yang table.

Windows of the store, open and closed. Turquoise and glass vessels. Layers of translucency. The cutout silhouette of a 1960s wall case is backlit by luminous drapes. The light from Soho softly diffuses around a worn, cerused Deco cabinet. The girl at her window. She is from the middle point between the eras of these two cabinets.

CHAPTER 10

ARTIST WORK

WEST BROADWAY LOFT

By the time Aero was heading into its second decade, my friend Laura was also becoming more established in her career as a professional artist and photographer in New York. She had moved out of her old Greenwich Village apartment and into a converted loft back in Soho. Laura eventually moved to a larger loft in this same building, just as I lived in two apartments in the same building on Sixtieth Street. Both of these places would cost a fortune today, but back then, if you were very lucky, you could find intact first-generation renovations of industrial loft space like this.

Her new home was right there on that legendary stretch of West Broadway that once was like the Fifth Avenue of the art world downtown, near the Leo Castelli gallery and so many others that we had frequented when we were younger. And really, for both of us, this time held something of a story about coming full circle. From our haunts and dreamed-of successes downtown during art school together, we had both left Soho and learned from different places and influences. I returned to build a business here. Laura chose to come back to Soho to live, in the kind of loft setting that we most associated with an artist's life of that period.

Like her Bethune Street apartment, I didn't decorate or renovate these lofts for Laura. This first one was a classic, fashionable loft apartment, and her second loft even more a true studio, both furnished in her eye; yet both are also continuing representations of what might be considered the modern Aero style. The idea of the creative, eclectic home, populated with collections and art, is the touchstone to so much of what I do, and a great deal of that comes from the loft idea: to recycle and revive old, found spaces in the spirit of an artist.

What I admire about this particular loft is its character. Most of the original structure is preserved within the late 1980s conversion that Laura inherited. It is a loft from that first residential boom in Soho and Tribeca, primarily a recalibration of the industrial building that had initially been there. And so, here is the familiar language of the archetypal New York loft apartment: the wall-sized large windows on one end, the durable rough-hewn wood floors, the high ceilings and brickwork, the structural columns. The newly added elements—for example, the metalyard cold-rolled steel partitions with their translucent glass panels used to carve out a bedroom––are part of that same vocabulary of industrial materials. Architecture from a factory past has been repurposed, freshened, and made domestic in the present.

Laura whitewashed her loft bright and clean, making it elegant and art-worthy almost instantly. But look closer and the unmatched windowpanes are of different generations, all still quirkily native to the building. The fire escape to the bustling Soho main street is part of the view. The timeworn wood floor is neither replaced nor refinished, but casually covered in a bound-sisal carpet, as if to convey the softer new reality of a home within the hard architecture of the space.

The facing walls of ever-so-simple, monumental bookshelves are the thing that I find most engaging here. The shelves were Laura's invention, made out of plain Canal Street hardware store brackets and long pine lumber boards. And even though there is absolutely nothing fancy about them, to me there is always a rich laboratory or library feeling that occurs when shelves cover a whole wall floor-to-ceiling, so practical and very elegant.

Such shelves particularly remind me of the studio of the artist I worked for during school. It was a classic painting loft, with the high, long, illuminated wall on which to set up large-scale canvases. Next to the work space was a storeroom, stacked with tidy and organized shelves of paints and other materials. I liked that juxtaposition of the big, open studio and the compact, adjacent storage room.

Laura used her shelves for the files and organization of her film work and her library of literature and art books, but her life here fits in that studio tradition. I chose the same type of high-ceilinged, industrial space for Aero for these same reasons. There would be that echo of an artist studio in the fourteen-foot walls and open rooms that I was filling with furniture and art. These places of Laura's and mine, with that

specific cultural history, do feel as if they could only be here in New York and from that moment in time.

Overall, this idea of loft living has a romance to it that I think remains primary in the minds of people coming to Soho to shop at Aero and other stores here. It has, for that customer and for the clients of my studio, perhaps always been about how to mix a hard-edged, industrial, urban environment with elegant collections and a finer manner of living. And, vice versa, it suggests how to bring something of that unvarnished, artistic, downtown world to a different kind of traditional environment that is not at all industrial.

The truth is that the uniqueness of living in this era of Soho is almost entirely gone. The loft tradition has now been exported to other gentrified industrial districts in countless other cities, including many other parts of New York. The loft building is a language all its own now: the large open plan with tall banks of windows, exposed columns, and a gently industrial palette of materials, cement, reclaimed wood, steel.

That is all the more reason to recall where loft style comes from, in a space like this one, so cleverly put together in harmony with a true old building.

The front of Laura's loft, looking out onto West Broadway between Prince and Spring Streets, in the heart of Soho. I am always struck by the charm of the mismatched old factory-era windows and the conspicuous fire escape that acted like a balcony. In other loft conversions of that time and undoubtedly today, this kind of architectural discord would be replaced with something more uniform, and less authentic.

Laura had one main space in which to create a modern live-work dwelling. The facing walls of shelves became the reinvention of her library, with the rows of archive boxes storing her film. This is an artist's workplace, yet the arrangement of books and the fine, colorful Gibbings desk at its center are a chic continuation of her collecting and taste. I refer to this favorite picture of the shelves, even today. Sometimes the simplest ideas, like plain bookshelves to cover rough brick walls, are the ones that create the most mystifying effect.

This loft was a half-floor unit, converted in a time when many of the huge, floor-through warehouses and stories of factory buildings in Soho were subdivided into smaller residences. The sole bedroom was carved out of the main area as a simple cube with sliding steel doors, their translucent panels forming a suggestion of Shoji screens. The clean steel beam in the center was likely a replacement for an original, more ornate cast-iron column, all very much in keeping with the stripped-back industrial language of materials used in these 1980s renovations. They can look quite dated today, but these lofts were an absolute invention of this location and time, in the new modern downtown. I think this one has an interesting point of inspiration, with some details that show thoughtfulness and subtlety.

The layout here is still more in the pattern of an artist's home than the expanded architectural world of residential loft living today. When I have designed lofts I am always mindful of how to connect new architecture to this character of what was there before. It's a different kind of history to live in, but the chapter here from the days of artists living downtown is part of what is so enchanting about these formally industrial and warehouse spaces of New York.

A view across the room to the facing wall of bookshelves. You can see the simple, bent-metal bookshelf brackets and thin lumberyard planks of the shelves, so rich when filled with on this grand scale. The biggest change from Laura's Bethune Street apartment is the great height of the space here. Lofts gave people this sense of spaciousness and height that was unique from other kinds of city apartments; that was a main part of their draw. And from the dark, enfolding colors of her small rooms in Greenwich Village, this one, big, high-ceilinged room lent itself to much more lightness and bright white—on the walls and cabinets, in the clean structure of a high-armed, boxy Donghia sofa in white, the white milk glass of the coffee table, the shearling rug on the sisal, the soft, light chenille on a vintage Italian chaise from Aero. On the other hand, Laura's favorite fiery orange remains the foil to all the white, especially in the row of bookcloth storage boxes under the bookshelves. As I remember, these boxes came from another shop in Soho, back when there were more home furnishings stores in the neighborhood.

Laura found these simple, prefab, panel-door cabinets in two graduated sizes, and used them to create a version of sideboard storage near her dining table. The top doubled as a gallery shelf for objects and art. I like her way of hanging pictures here: loose and sporadic, almost like a collage, and very much in character with the artwork itself. Often I hang art like this, in a casual organization that seems to build spatially as pieces are added; other times, I fit pieces together in a tighter, more formal grid. Both are modern ways of handling a salon-style organization for art.

Pure, bold colors are continually of interest to Laura, and even in this new white loft there is a celebration of color that is really vibrant. The set of Limoges china is a unique thing that she put together, by selecting and coordinating the different pieces in this group of colors she likes. The earliest classes we took together in art school were on color theory, and the primary hues of the china in their pretty stacks do make me think of the color exercises we did back then.

Laura loved and has always kept this slightly broken Giò Ponti chair from Aero. This is another one of those worn, elegiac antiques that I am always collecting, and which I am inclined to leave as they are. With pieces that need restoration, among all the chairs and chandeliers, lamps and table bases that I buy, I'm always pressed about what to take on and make pristine again. But sometimes an old thing is intact and beautiful enough to be left in its disrepair in a more surprising and charming way. Laura and I connect on this level of the found object, much as in school, we were finding things on the street to make art with. And even though it is from a renowned designer, and had once been finely gessoed and gilded, this chair in its state of ruin is like a type of found art. Flecks of red clay and gilding survive on the bow-like motif of the back, while the rest of the frame is like a mantelpiece that's been partially scraped. The torn leather seat has a dark shadow where it was once repaired with tape. The chair is like a reflection of some of the older parts of the loft in that way: both are remnants of another history.

This is Fang, the daughter of my cat, Emma. When I first rescued Emma she was pregnant but so tiny, barely more than a kitten herself. At that time in school, I was working as a bartender at the nightclub Area. Area was the artistic hub and most theatrical of all the downtown clubs that were the big scene back then. It was best known for its changing, eccentric visual themes that would run for about six weeks at a time. There was a long hallway of dioramas that you walked past when entering into the main club space, and these would be redecorated along with the rest of the halls and rooms for every theme change. Many of those installations were created by up-and-coming artists, always with such precision and originality. They were like looking at wonderful window displays in the city. That summer when I found Emma, Area was in a theme called Sports. We also sometimes had specific party nights, and during Sports, one such party night happened to be called Pets. I brought Emma and her new kittens down for an evening to be art stars in their own protected croquet window, behind glass. After that, Laura chose Fang out of all the kittens, and the rest were adopted by other artists and Area coworkers. And Emma, the most wonderful, mellow, maternal cat, lived for twenty-two more years.

CHAPTER 11

UPSTAIRS DOWNSTAIRS

SHOP DETAILS

As early as 1993 I knew that we needed more space, more shelves, more infrastructure at Aero. Literally we needed a real cash register and a place to wrap things, to manage the sale of accessories and stocked goods in this store that was being created.

That year, a small storefront next door to our Spring Street entrance became available. It had been a toy store, with a toy bear outside on the sidewalk that blew bubbles all day long. Many people traveled downtown to shop there, and it was very much a neighborhood loss when it suddenly closed. By 1994, the space was ours to be the downstairs Aero shop.

Having a storefront on Spring Street gave us a street-level window in which to do all kinds of special and seasonal displays. I could carry more houseware and accessories—things for the kitchen and for entertaining, a bigger mix of vintage, new, imported, and local New York–made items. I compiled dining and servingware, pillows and throws, collectibles, vessels, baskets and trays, deskware, and small antiques. It was a different and much more mercantile venture than the quiet studio mood of the gallery upstairs, and in the early years of Aero, it was really a thing I fought hard to bring to life.

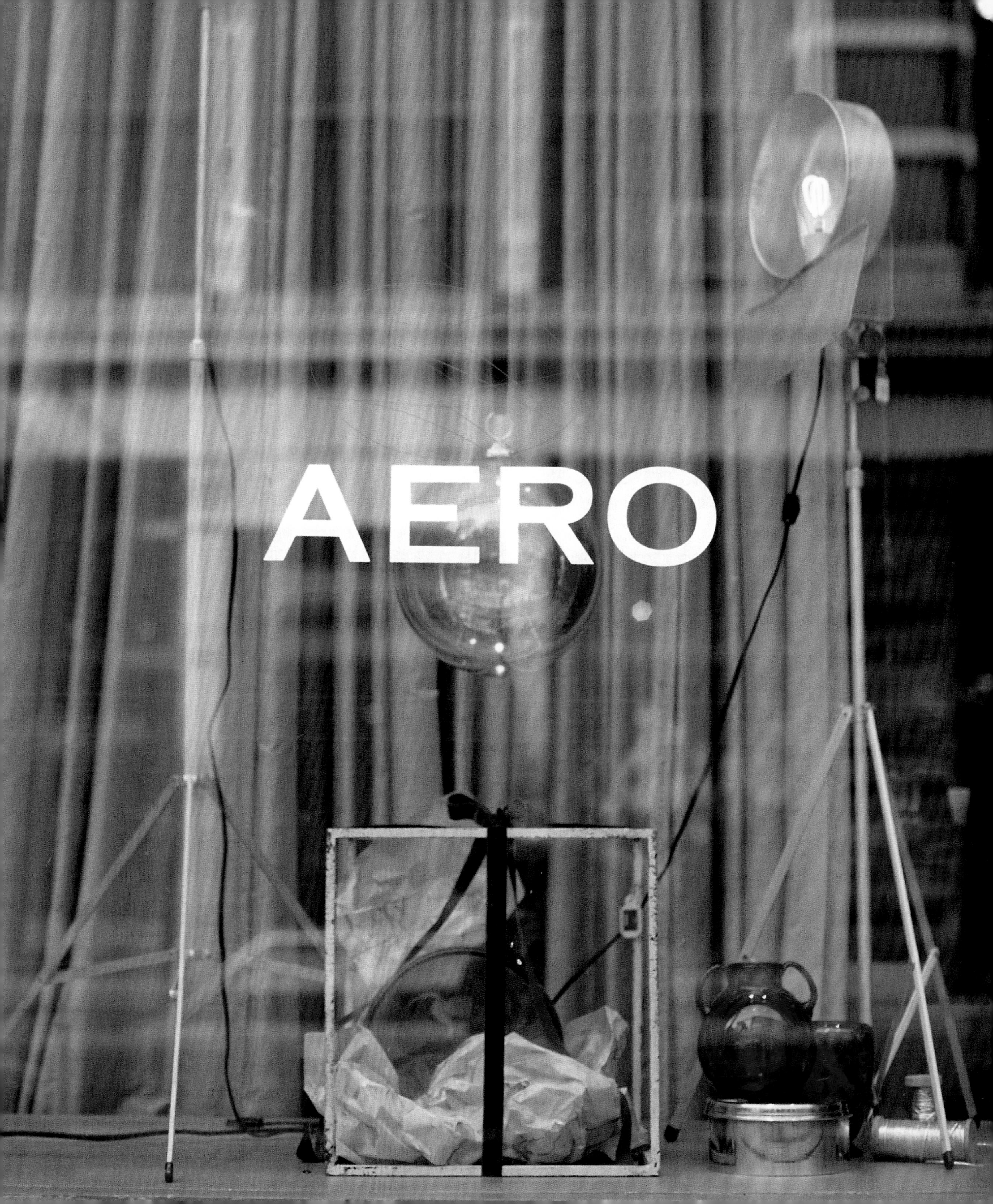
AERO

As the years have passed, I've added my own product collections of furniture, lighting, bedding, carpets and textiles, dishes, glass and barware, and tabletop items, on top of the goods I buy from craftspeople or find on antiquing runs.

These things aren't props. They are equal parts of what I think of as the Aero home. Moreover, they are and have always been, certainly in my own collecting, a means to establishing a style when bigger investments in furniture and art are out of reach. I have always believed in having the range of these goods as the foundation of what is needed to furnish, live in, and make actual households special.

In many ways, as the downstairs shop developed, it represented the missing piece of Aero. The slender railroad dimensions of the space felt like a version of the old antique stores that I have always stopped into, full of good things to be discovered. I often tell stories about how I used to stay at Aero late into the night, after sketching and designing in the studio, and later stocking goods in the store myself, bringing our limited merchandise up from the basement, styling the windows. But I loved it. It was an important moment that set other pieces of my future with Aero into motion.

I wanted a modern playfulness as well as practicality in the design of the downstairs store, especially in the fabrication of all the fixtures and cases. At the back wall I used large-scale industrial metal piping with custom brackets and thick Lucite shelves, like the slabs I'd bought down at Canal

Street during school to use for sculpture projects. I have always loved the resinous, softly transparent look of Lucite cut very thick. For another wall I designed modular, stackable cubbies in grey and marigold paint colors and different wood finishes that we also sold as furniture. I designed the first of my Aero trays to hold the tissue paper at our register. The oversized worktable that I designed as our cash wrap went on to be the model for a number of kitchen islands I designed for clients.

I always think about store design in a very residential way. Home is where my ideas come from. I'm really never happier than when I'm working in my kitchen surrounded by my favorite cookbooks and supplies, or when I am organizing the rooms of my house. And there are those times when I entertain and make more of an event of my home for guests. This Aero shop was about that intersection of domestic and public selves, and presenting the world of goods that I would want for my clients and for my own home—everything from how cabinets and shelves are built to what items we use daily, what variety of objects we're drawn to, what qualities they have, what refinement.

I think that domesticity flows into other stores that I've been hired to design over the years for the fashion and home brands I've worked with. I want to build individual character into certain details of construction, lighting, choice of materials. And home is at the root of my relationships with the companies for whom I create products. These merchants all visited Aero; they all came to me through the things that I was doing at this store, upstairs and downstairs.

So, it has not been uncommon for a fixture or a light or a piece of cabinetry that I've designed for a store to be reworked as a product for Aero, or vice versa; just as an antique that I restore might be the inspiration for a new piece of furniture that I design. Stores do become a unique outlet and inspiration in this ongoing collaboration with the things I want to make. They are all parts of the same story.

As one who likes to collect dishes, I made a big commitment to carry a stock of this classic French, white-glazed, eighteenth-century-style china at Aero. It was so stylish, and a nice thing to sell in larger numbers for entertaining. A 1960s executive desk serves as a table. Oftentimes the vintage furniture that comes into the store may be outmoded or out of scale for today's homes, so we repurpose the pieces for different uses than they were originally made for. There are unique inventions of manufactured bar cabinets, desks, wardrobes, secretaries, sideboards, and dressing tables going back to the 1930s and '40s, with interesting details worth saving. A piece like the low drop-front secretary, above, could serve as an entrance cabinet in an apartment foyer, or as a small sideboard. New York apartments always require such multi-functional pieces of furniture.

This shadowy photo, taken at dusk, shows a richer, textured, dark set of silhouettes that sometimes comes together in a corner of the store. There are certain architectural, blocky pieces of furniture from the 1940s and earlier that I tend to find or refinish in darker colors, and that's where this mood comes from. The setting includes my old Chanel sofa, its leather darkened by wax and exposure to sunlight. The giant trunk basket was an expensive one to buy for the store, especially relative to many other baskets and objects. But I chose it, as I always look for this sort of new and different piece to use as an unusual coffee table or ottoman, with the upholstery of a clubby living room or den. Above, a detail of a rich, masculine, bedroom study that I designed in leather and ebonized wood. The cabinetry idea came from a 1940s side table with the same geometric, integrated handles.

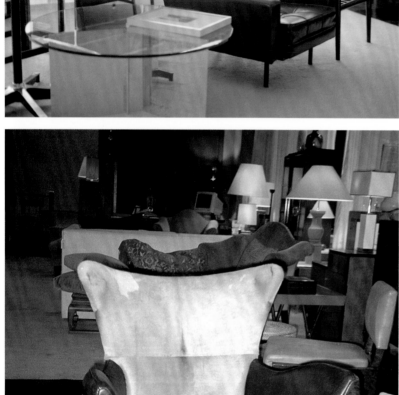

Later modern club chairs and an earlier 1930s tubular desk chair. 1950s boxy lines; 1960s sculpted curves and wings. All are in Aero leather, calfskin, and mohair.

These are the sorts of vintage modern armchairs that I like to find for a sitting room, study, or library. When deciding how to refurbish each chair, I consider what's clubby, upright, paired, or individual, and where I envision the piece going. With these ideas in mind, I will often split up a set of dining chairs to create a special pair of desk chairs, composed of an armchair and a side, two armchairs, or even two sides. The favorite Paul McCobb California Modern chair is one of a divided set that eventually came home with me. Today it is harder and harder to find wonderful small Deco club chairs like this narrow-armed example. The sleek 1960s chrome-bolted ottoman was dressed up in button-tufted charcoal brown leather.

An often-used favorite: Nympheus block print from Lee Jofa, upholstered on an antique Swedish side chair.

Dining chairs from the 1940s often have the most inventive, sculptural upholstery. Sometimes I like to use a formally patterned or unusual fabric with these interesting silhouettes. A Fortuny damask print and studded nailheads; turquoise green shagreened leather; a coordinated arm and side chair with witty cutout backs.

Detailed and unique. An ebonized, 1960s open-arm chair with vintage Pucci printed lamb suede. Ultra-fine caning on an Italian classical side chair. A 1940s skyscraper-back armchair. Alternating nailhead sizes on a 1940s side chair.

For a client's wood-paneled dining room, I made a set of lampshades from a series of nineteenth-century sepia museum photo plates. This is of one of the faces of Botticelli's *Primavera*.

I am always searching for intricate, unusual, and decorative chairs that are winning on their own. A fanciful, elaborate English Chinoiserie pagoda armchair. A tall-back, mini-tufted Tommi Parzinger dining chair. Wonderful round cutouts on a little Scandinavian kitchen chair.

Table geometries: trestle, hexagon, cantilevered.

197

Low tables: smoked glass and tapered aluminum, radial pattern French tile.

Vintage and modern: tiered center table in pale honey cerused oak.

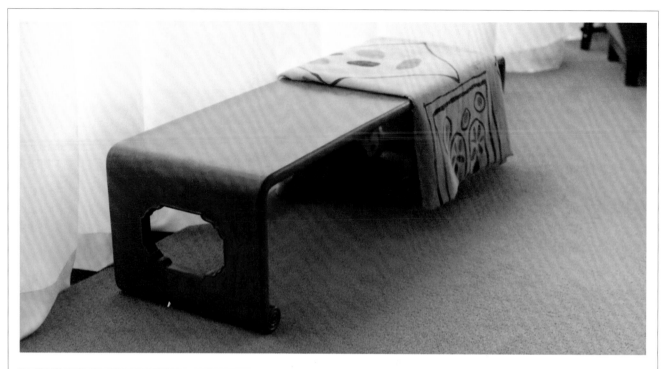

Chinese modern elegance. Nail-mended, primitive beauty on a two-tier wire leg folk stool.

These are the only pictures that I know of from the opening party for the downstairs street-level shop. The grainy, rushed exposures remind me of the excitement of that very big moment, but all these years later, there is no real record of this event in the life of the store. Of the two spaces, the upstairs gallery had its own dressy elegance, while downstairs was meant to be more casual, fun, and colorful—a modern Scandinavian walnut wing chair upholstered in an American rag rug, or a found pair of slipper chairs painted pastel yellow and pink. These two I covered in a fabric mill's sample "blanket" that showed bands of potential colorways for a specific textile, a very hard-to-find thing in all of my years of antiquing. I'm so glad to have captured the chairs here because they sold immediately, and I've always wondered where they went. I do wish I had a better picture of them.

The shop had one street-level window that was open to the store with a drape to one side. This is a picture of one of the first furniture groupings just inside of that window. I designed the folding, whitewashed, framed panel screen to be filled with matted photo plates from a worn nineteenth-century portfolio of museum paintings that I had found. I had used Botticelli prints for other projects, while for this piece I chose Titian and Velazquez paintings. For the downstairs shop I was also scouting and buying more contemporary, well-made international accessories and deskware, including Scandinavian raw teak as well as a number of Japanese bronze objects and candlesticks that we still sell versions of today. These new and modern items married into a mix of vintage and junk-shop finds from my ever-constant antiquing. Here I added a few Italian modernist floor lamps by Joe Colombo, still a constant for the store whenever I come across them. So this mix of old and new was what the shop was. I can't help loving both worlds.

Besides my own Aero lamps, vintage lamps always filtered through the shop. Then as now, I pick up driftwood lamps whenever I find them; some are kept natural, others are gessoed or gilded. The modular Keith shelf units were created to stack up as shelving for display. We also sold them as individual side tables. The fun was in the many different finishes that the form could be made in, from maple, mahogany, oak, or walnut, to brightly colored lacquers and our own Aero white rub. I still use the maple ones from the shop today in our new studio, to hold all of our auction catalogs.

The uplit metal corner shelf, to the right, became the basis for the shelving that lines the front of the current Aero store on Broome Street. I like the vintage medical cabinet look of the plate glass on the painted white frame, and most of all, that the shelves were welded and fixed so that the frame stayed light and thin. That decision gave the shelves a much more elegant, residential, permanent feeling. I am also amused to see the little terra-cotta pots of citronella candles in this picture. Aero probably was not the place that people thought to come to buy garden candles, so they rarely sold, and I finally brought them home. So many years later, I still have them in my garden. They never seem to burn down.

On these pages are some of my very earliest product designs. To the left, examples from a set of still-lifes that I photographed, presenting the mood and character of a glassware collection for Tiffany & Co. The images included my technical drawings of individual pieces in the collection, along with some of my own antiques that had inspired them—opal and mercury glass, stemware with elegant turnings and banded motifs, things of diminutive, precious detail. For me, the photos are artistic favorites, with their modern, soft blue light and opalescent tones. The tray below is one of those fine modern pieces of 1920s metalwork that may look simple, but is really so poetically engineered and handmade of beautiful materials. Probably nowhere is the influence of this type of antique modern design more evident than in the lighting that has become such a big part of Aero. Here are the first three Aero store limited-production lamps, in cobalt-blue glass and bookcloth.

I always like geometric cylinders and globes for lamps. The milk glass columns are a first-generation Aero product: I bought a dozen or so of these cylinders and had them made into lamps with raw wood bases. Years later I commissioned hand-blown clear glass cylinders in the same lamp form. This one magnifies the view out the window at the corner of Wooster and Spring Streets.

The 1930s industrial set light on a pivoting yoke stand is an absolute, all-time favorite. I love the mechanical details in everything from the piercings in the shade to the clamp on the neck to the flourish of the bolt, almost like a classical turning.

Like many designers before me, I am always searching for intriguing, sculptural forms, antique or new, to turn into lamp bases. Here is one we made out of a patinated tin starburst. The raw wood turning is an early Aero design. I managed to get it made in small runs of six or eight pieces at a time, together with one or two other forms that were turned for me by a talented frame-maker at a special custom upholstery workroom. The tall, curving, triform rattan lamp and moody ceramic globe lamp are both vintage finds with new custom shades.

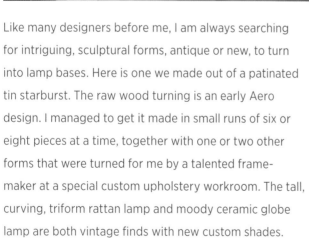

In the shop downstairs, the doors to our tiny back office were made with heavy gauge, industrial wire mesh over glass. We custom-painted a giant JetStream ceiling fan, from my favorite industrial hardware catalog, and we still sell these today. A 1970s tapered wire stand holds a blackened terra cotta vessel, like a geometric Brancusi studio object, a beautiful, elegant shadow. Sometimes I choose a piece just for its silhouette, because it's sculptural and wonderful to look at.

CHAPTER 12

CHANGING LOFT

WEST BROADWAY, UPSTAIRS

Laura's friends always used to say that she had the apartment luck. This is certainly true of the wonderful homes she has found (or that find her), including the houses in countryside areas where she has spent time outside of the city. I have admired Laura's free spirit and luck in life as she has come and gone on her many travels over the years, even as I've been much more tied to the world of New York, with my company and store and the studio. Sometimes I wish I had a bit more of that traveling life, finding and discovering new things along the way.

But at least part of Laura's luck must also be style. In each place she settles, she is able to shape something that immediately looks like the best example of what that place should be. This is the case with the larger full-floor loft that she lived in upstairs in her building on West Broadway.

In this upstairs loft Laura had enough room to create a complete live-work space. She finally had her own studio at home—not only for her still-life photography, but also for making other types of fine art.

Not long before this move, Laura had been renting a weekend house in Connecticut. There she had started a new body of work in the form of graphite drawings on paper and canvas. I remember I was so intrigued by these images, which were abstract and graphic but incredibly delicate. Having always sold her photographs at Aero, I felt it was important to have a show of this work. We did, in 2007, and I continue to sell these pieces as well as Laura's photography.

At the same time she was making these drawings, Laura was also manipulating large, blown-up and abstracted architectural photographs into saturated color prints. As she funneled more of these colors into her art, certain choices she made in her surrounding grew more subtle. All of this shows in the studio identity she created in this loft.

One of the interesting shifts in this direction is the shiny white painted floor that runs continuously through the space. As I had come to favor white floors at home and used a glossy nautical-feeling paint to this effect in my house on Long Island, Laura and I chose the same paint and used it to create an airy white envelope for her studio and living space. The fresh white walls and floors give this loft a complete finish and sophistication. In another way, the continuity of that white connects the suggested room areas and keeps the space feeling like the big, open loft it is. Considering this space as one in a series of Laura's homes, I do love the romantic idea of the turn-of-the-century artist loft that culminates in her modern studio life here.

And as in a studio, with its high, long walls, the art is hung more loosely. Laura's own art is larger, and the subject matter is more mixed, between portraits, landscapes, still lifes, and colorful abstract works. I think it all captures the ease of the creative mindset here—nothing too formal or filled up.

Consequently, some of her old furniture is used to different ends, and this space being bigger, Laura added a few more pieces to create a new living room area. She chose one of the larger, deep, tailored sofas that I had recently designed and upholstered it in natural linen. A huge floor lamp from Aero was made from a rolling photography mounting stand, combined with a custom drum shade; one of the early examples of this kind of set light made residential. Together we found a pair of great 1960s Italian laced leather and wood sling chairs on an antiquing trip up to Hudson, New York.

There are also the practical solutions of Laura's work life in this studio. In our foundation year at the Cooper Union, the two of us had a period of time when we painted together on the same paintings, and we shared space in one small corner of a studio. This space reminds me of that. There is the wall of seamless paper and her easel in a corner of the loft. Here are Laura's edited bookshelves, holding her now-extended archive of film, all carefully stored in elegant, parchment-colored file boxes, a sculpture of organization. And in these boxes is an entire world of work. All of the film that constituted my first book, which Laura photographed, lives in these boxes, as well as much other film that she sorted through to share with me in this book.

We live in a world now where a whole library of books, a music collection, and a repository of photographs can all be stored on a device smaller than one of those archive boxes. But I would make a plea just as well for preserving and exhibiting the individual physical evidence of creative endeavors. I love having a library of books at home and at work. I love knowing that there is an actual archival library of film in these boxes in Laura's loft.

And yet there is no question that things do evolve. Here, those boxes sit above a double desk that speaks of a new expansion in the story, and new beginnings. Laura's daughter Tessa, my goddaughter, was born during the years pictured in this loft. She changed the math of how to live in the city, how to raise a family, and in what kind of home.

Laura has always had the home luck, and she has always been a traveler. During the making of this book she has been living with her family in northern California, and she continues to split her time between New York and the West Coast. Lately some of my projects have been taking me to California, too. And so we get to meet sometimes in this new place. I visit Tessa when I can, and I see how much Laura is enjoying being in California. It is a different, whole view of America, in everything from the architecture to the food. And because of these trips, I've discovered other places, from the rolling hills and unbelievably beautiful, preserved

coastline to the color and silence of redwood forests. For someone like me who is interested in landscape and gardening, seeing this other side of the country has been inspiring and fulfilling.

And in this time, after all, I am becoming a traveler, too.

Entering Laura's loft, upstairs on West Broadway. The stairwell leads to the roof. The Tommi Parzinger cabinet that previously lived in Laura's bedroom now becomes an entry cabinet. The very large Pyrex glass laboratory cylinder by its side is an Aero staple that I have carried in the store for many years. A roll of orange acetate is evidence of the world of the artist living in this space: something that Laura would have used for filters in the new photography she was doing. Looking at this view into the big, open, full-floor room, with its subtle divisions of living areas and even its distinctive pair of chairs, I am reminded more than anywhere else in this book of how much this looks like the early Aero—the all-essential loft.

The living room zone, tucked across from the office, is defined by a wall of art. The large-scale tinted photograph is one of Laura's color works that she was doing at this time. The pieces are hung more loosely, with art going up and coming down in the rhythm of a working studio.

I do like how Laura made something special out of the plain, inherited, open corner kitchen, with its Formica counters and generic white cabinets and the 1980s classic Lightolier can lights. What's unique here is the great, raw, industrial iron grille on the skylight, a benefit of being on the top floor. We paired that open skylight square with a large-scale, moonlike Noguchi paper lantern that floated above the round Aalto table. The table and chairs are very low-slung in the classic Scandinavian way; even the Ikea wooden dish rack has a woody, modern simplicity that comes from the world of Aalto. I also like the line of open cupboards without an upper course, leaving room for art to lean on top. The shelves hold many accumulated bits and pieces of the Aero store through the years, along with new tableware that I was designing around this time for Marshall Field's. Laura loved her set of Clair dishes from that collection, with their soft, antique creamware color in her modern, white, loft kitchen.

In the double-office setup, the memorable floor-to-ceiling shelves of the previous loft have been lifted above two desks: one belonging to Laura and the other to her partner, Cloud Devine, also a photographer. All the books are removed now to make room for a growing archive of film and prints. I love the unique placement of the shelf of CDs at eye level. Rather than hide media away in an armoire or entertainment closet, this is an open collection of the type of art and music that Laura and Cloud lived with. The space is about them, revealing what they do and how they work, in a way that is so nice, true, and unstaged. Nothing is precious and no style is lost in the selection of furnishings, mixing modern antiques—the Eames chairs, a 1930s Kurt Versen lamp—with the 1990s newness of practical Ikea desks. Even the simple clip-on work lights from Canal Hardware function in such a chic, interesting way, with such a good shape. I still remember them creating just the right soft light at the edge of this big room.

In Laura's studio, a roll of seamless is set up for photography and an easel holds one of her graphite drawings. She developed the layered detail of these drawings both on the easel and by rubbing her materials into the canvas or paper as it lay flat on the worktable.

The Gilbert Rohde cabinet that stored her china on Bethune Street is repurposed as a bookcase in the sitting area of the studio. I remember when I first got this piece in at Aero. Deco-era furniture of this sort is often brown or black in its original finish. This one was brown with silver paint. And just as I'm inclined to darken a lot of honey-colored modern and Danish teak furniture, here I did the reverse: I lightened the cabinet with ochre Japan paint and had it refinished with a red lacquer interior.

These bookcases forming a type of bed niche were part of the loft when Laura moved in. I remember us discussing what to do with this problematic wall and its odd configuration of thick, flat-fronted shelves, but Laura's way of organizing her books and magazines here is really handsome and sensible. Some special furnishings also helped to soften all that architecture around the bed. We found the pair of unique, vintage Saarinen tables on a shopping trip upstate. The tall candlestick lamps are Aero-made. The textile behind the bed is African, from the old Craft Caravan store in Soho, where we both used to shop.

Looking back, I am struck by this modern bedroom filled with literature, and how rich and peaceful it is. The library bedroom is such a rarity nowadays, but it is something deserving of a revival.

CHAPTER 13

TO BROOME STREET

AERO TODAY

By 2000 or 2001, with the Spring Street store busy and the design studio growing overcrowded, I first began considering the reality that I needed to move Aero to a larger space. This turn of events happened to coincide with the time when I had moved from my Brookhaven cottage and was restoring my current house on Long Island. New ideas were percolating through that process, especially about more refined American neoclassical and English Georgian architecture. I was designing a new furniture collection in this direction, and using elements of those historical styles in several of the client homes I was working on. Aero has always been my modern counterweight to those traditional leanings. And so not just for more room, but also to implement new design, it began to seem time for a reinvention of Aero as well.

In late 2003, I found a large, street-level storefront on Broome Street, with a high-ceilinged cellar level connected by an open stairway. This space became the new home of Aero in the summer of 2004 and we are still there today.

Central Soho was certainly changing by this time. The fashion boutiques were moving in while the antique and home stores were moving out. It's partly that dissolution of what Soho had been that made me dig my heels in more, to preserve the kind of independent curated store that Aero was to the neighborhood. Since those days, young proprietors and entrepreneurs have moved away and started up elsewhere, in Nolita or in Brooklyn, and even points outside the city like upstate in Hudson, New York. That made keeping Aero going right here all the more important. I wanted to stay downtown.

On the outskirts of the neighborhood, up at Crosby Street, this late-blooming pocket of Soho has a familiar edge. It has attracted a very nice mix of smaller merchants and boutiques. One still feels the buzz and messy commercial pull of Canal Street nearby.

While Aero on Spring Street was perched in a smaller, reconditioned Art Deco structure, this new space is front and center in one of the neighborhood's 1870s cast-iron buildings. The ground floor is simply a long and wide floor-through loft. It has the contradiction of its original rough brick walls and ornate Corinthian columns, plus a classic loft skylight in the back. The space has those studio bones, with its emblematic skylight and big, open room.

And so I've switched parts of the old Aero configuration to make the best use of the Broome Street loft. The design studio has moved downstairs, below the main street-level shop. Our conference room where I work most of the day with all of the design staff is located at the rear of the main floor, under that skylight, visible but still secreted behind a most striking set of doors. I designed these new doors to be dramatically tall and narrow, fourteen feet high, painted high-gloss jet black. The Aero studio still lives inside the Aero store.

With this large, classic loft, I've had an opportunity to invent a new beginning for Aero, but now with a more mature enterprise, a look, a completely new architecture. I admit it is a rather special circumstance for a designer who is in the business of creating spaces for others to have more than one chance to build a world of his own, with a clean slate and no constraints.

I looked to my own artistic roots and interests in the essence of the art studio as a design theme for this space. Ideas came from books and vintage photos of the studios of favorite artists working through the 1920s in Europe. The new store references the colors and screen partitions from Paul Klee's 1927 painting studio, along with the studios of Brancusi and Mondrian, Pierre Chareau's Maison de Verre in Paris, and functionalist houses by Adolf Loos. I admire these early modern spaces for the way their craftsmanship bridges older traditions, but their design favors newer properties of material and architecture. This is how I wanted to build Aero— exposed structure and joinery, cases and ledges to hold objects, great flow of light, a simple and flexible space that is beautifully made.

And these combined ideas—the Anglo-American and the European, the different depths of field in architecture and photography, the shared purity in Georgian and modernist design—have remained interests of mine and themes in my work over many years.

The Broome Street space has been my constant window onto this new equation. And the store in particular, with its high walls of densely stocked shelves and its series of suggested rooms, continues on in new and layered ways. The size of it feels much more like an old emporium or even a general store, which I like. To be sure, there is a piece of the old store here that has been carried along, in certain ideas of the fixturing and in the upstairs-downstairs exchange of studio and store. But in pictures especially, something changes as we settle into the new Aero.

NEW EYES

I have been so lucky over the years to have talented creative people of many disciplines come to work at Aero. There have been musicians, writers, chefs, teachers, clothes-makers, and woodworkers among the designers and architects and the store staff. One such person is photographer Michelle Arcila. She came to Aero as my assistant several years ago, but to me, she is one who always creates, an absolute artist.

During her years at Aero, Michelle took many pictures for the store, from still lifes to candid portraits at Aero events and parties. Just as my friend Laura photographed the Aero of Spring Street, Michelle has documented Broome Street. I'm a collector of her fine photography. Like Laura's, I sell her work at Aero.

Michelle takes very modern and prolific photos that do have the more spontaneous feeling of the digital camera of this age, as compared to the temperament and timing of film. There is a liberating spirit to this photography that is helping to define what feels modern and crafted at Aero in the time of now. As a record of the store, the resulting pictures are more a live document than the many product shots and atmospheric scenes that we would more carefully stage for photoshoots in the early years. Michelle finds the picture that is there, waiting in the arrangement of things as they are, casually observed but nonetheless revealing, joyful, and lyrical.

The work of Michelle taking pictures is now simply part of making the store, always keeping in mind the point of view of the shopper. She captures some of the vitality of this place that I hope people do feel when they visit Aero.

And so here are some glimpses of the way the store has truly looked on any given day, the way the baskets were stacked or the art hung. A cluster of items on a shelf, a grouping of wood or porcelain or glass; a collection displayed as it might come together in someone's home. Made-to-order furniture is mixed with vintage pieces, as I would combine those items in a residence. It all shows just how I put together things on a continuing basis.

There is nothing terribly spare about any of this. More accurately, this Aero is full, even maximal. But there is something modern in the cacophony, too. For all the variety of goods are filtered together by color, or material, or a chosen theme. Fullness can be one kind of modern, and the store in its way is just as edited as ever, even though there is more to see.

And all these ingredients make up the real portrait of the Aero that is here today.

A view into the front of the store. This is the Aero of today. Shop goods and shelves of homeware are reunited with vintage furniture, art, and more of my own designed furnishings, all together in one giant loft. Sometimes in this store we have the spareness and procession of room sets that resemble the original Aero. Other times the store is dense and literally piled up with goods, the furniture lined up along narrow aisleways like an auction house or streetscape. The span of original brick wall behind the stairs is fitted with a system of picture rails for hanging art. In this particular setting is a pair of elegantly tall, 1940s graphic panel cabinets that we refurbished with a matte-grey wash on the gridded door fronts, white gold-leaf handles, and polished mahogany on the outer case. My Nicola carpet is based on an antique jacquard damask textile and made of modern jute and hemp. The large, steel architectural light is an especially fine example of a 1930s building uplight that we had restored and replated in nickel.

Hand-made and machine-made. My perpetual collection of industrial lamps and objects is interspersed among the handicrafts and all the handblown glass in the store. The thermal photograph of my hand is part of a fascinating series of hand "portraits," made by my friend, artist Gary Schneider. Also by Gary are the prints of nineteenth-century slices of botanical specimens that he discovered and preserved, so modern and almost stellar in form, arranged between the tall doors to the conference room beyond.

There are shadows of light and dark and a beautiful depth of field in the combination of chocolate, celadon, and cream. The 1960s chairs are reinvented in crocodile-embossed leather, with tailored nailheads, darkened frames, and repatinated tapering feet. My Calliope ivory silk and wool carpet is based on a vintage Dorothy Thorpe etched glass pattern. Above, I designed a grid of square, polished walnut bookcases to follow the stairs that lead down from the front of the store to the lower-level shop and the design studio. The cases are quite often filled with the rich world of Japanese ceramics, wood, and bronze that has been a touchstone for me since the beginning of Aero.

Diverse art and modern fabric motifs merge with more traditional English elements at this gallery wall. I designed the Atheneum sofa as the update of a Regency-style divan that could be a more formal anchor in a room like a library or conservatory. The marble coffee table follows the spare inlaid pattern of a Georgian panelized stone-top pier table. The tall ebonized and gilded mirror is Victorian, and in front of it stands a finely carved neoclassical mahogany pedestal. A bamboo easel gilded in white gold leaf holds another piece of art, salon style. Modernism appears in the Deco-style club chairs that are upholstered in my Morocco pattern chenille, a pairing inspired by Yves St. Laurent. But the woodiness and masculinity of the colors feels of the Aero world. Layers of mocha, gold, and deep brown occur from the wavy taupe lines of the Fiona pattern chenille on the sofa, to the chocolate, Deco-inspired carpet beneath. Pale grey paint on the brick and the opal luster of alabaster and rock crystal add light and tranquility. The rich, collected mood is a recent reflection of many of the things I am interested in.

I am always looking for the simple, modern geometries of objects, in a collection of globes and spheres, or the cones and pyramids of lamp bases. I am also inclined to assemble the store based on groupings of color. I like black and blue together, smoky grey and taupe. Above, I commissioned artist Carol Leskanic to gild a pair of vintage tot-sized school chairs, and she turned them into whimsical artworks with her signature raised gesso dot motifs. A trio of antique-style, cast zinc rabbits from Japan perches on top of one of our vintage display cabinets filled with baby gifts. I started our small baby department buying turn-of-the-century children's bowls, and from there a collection has grown that is very special and defining for me in the point of view of the store. The photograph, *Dutch Light*, is by Michelle Arcila.

Woven variations. Fields and borders become a graphic idea in a laced cowhide rug; my Academy twill weave on a chair with contrasting piping; dark modernist porcelain with pinstripe platinum banding. The grain of wood and leather; tree limbs made into boxes. And baskets, baskets, baskets. There are very few stores left in New York City where you can find an assortment of good-quality and inventive baskets. I am constantly buying them as I find them, part of an ever-vigilant hunt. I honestly buy too many, and baskets are bulky and hard to store, so this is one of my favorite ways to display them, all in a mountain, with their different weaves and tones.

Hunting and gathering. The cases in the store are always filled with a mix of accessories, tableware, antiques, small artworks, and items for entertaining. I buy newer things in small sets as though they are vintage, and most often sell them individually. One of the pleasures of putting this collection together every season is the international flavor it brings. Objects come from local craft traditions in China, Japan, India, France, eastern Europe, and the United States. Elements that are constants for me: sets of glasses, opal glass, teapots and cups, candlesticks and vases, Japanese kitchenware. I love watery blue accents and glazed porcelain. Essentially I end up creating a shop with the peculiar variety of items that I collect for my own home, and reciprocally, antique pieces from home do make their way back to these shelves.

Two-tone worlds. I still like to find ways for dark and more masculine things to be soft, rich, and smoky. This notion is a favorite for me and I think customers, too. We did a smoky grey finish on a 1960s chest of drawers with a darker cabinet frame. That grey has become a standard Aero tone like our translucent whitewash finishes earlier on. The strapped bamboo chair was darkened and reupholstered in a great, neutral 1970s African fabric. This mid-century teak screen becomes much more interesting and luxurious with the addition of randomly gessoed or gilded panels in white gold leaf.

The art of black and white. With all the lamp light in the store, and especially into the evenings, Aero sometimes feels like a series of black-and-white photographs in its layers of light and dark. There is a patina to photographic black and white that is even more subtle when taking pictures of pictures, a subject I've been fascinated with since school. I am committed to showing artwork of all types in this store, in rotating arrangements that encourage people to collect and gather pieces over time. This is what inspired me to paint one alcove black in the Broome Street space, following Paul Klee's black-walled Bauhaus painting studio in the 1920s. You can see any kind of art very clearly and elegantly on a black background, sometimes even more than on white.

I have designed several secretary cabinets over the years. This is a type of antique furniture that I grew up with and certainly saw at country auctions when I was young. A secretary still speaks to me of a tradition of collection and display, sharing interests and souvenirs of travels, all around a desk where one writes: the found and the learned together. The two different examples here are also interesting in that they reverse dark and light. My Hallings secretary on the left has 1940s French influences, with an antique ivory finish on the exterior and dark kingwood and leather inside. The Hugo cabinet desk is based on a turn-of-the-century Norwegian highboy, with a mahogany case and an ivory interior.

Floor to ceiling, in city style. In the back of the store, the doors to the conference room stand fourteen feet high. I'd long saved and obsessed over an image of very flat, vintage, tall doors, and this location was the right place to use the idea in a sleek, urbanized way. The custom version of my 1920s-inspired Alium carpet was made for the opening of the store, based on another tiny auction image that I'd saved since my Polo days and had always wanted to make. Dark navy velvet, a streamlined chandelier, an antique map of Manhattan, the skyscraper proportions: all ingredients in the cosmopolitan vision of New York that this store embodies.

Variations in the store window: night and day, color and non-color, tie-dye and neoclassical, sculpture and light. I think of the windows we create as mini-sets of imagined moments. Breakfast in bed. Cocktails. A sparkling white, retro city office. We've had a teepee, a butcher block table, a profusion of crystal. Aero gets to be all these things and anything else I can dream up that will enchant. One time in the old store I bought twelve pairs of cast-iron bear bookends for a Christmas window. Everyone thought it was a little crazy at first but the scene was charming and we sold them all. The bears have become an ever-popular mascot of the store and here they are in another window on Broome Street.

MY OWN WAY

AT THE ACADEMY

Much of the pleasure in design is in the long game: watching how an object or an interior is a living, ongoing thing over time. Sometimes the constituents are meant to stay in the same arrangement, but more often they move and recombine and mate with newcomers in different ways over the years. You don't really see the longevity or the heart of an idea, after all, until you have lived with it and can know how it still surprises you. Giving time to observation is how you find things to believe in.

Taking pictures can be a similar process, providing a new perspective on familiar subjects over time.

In these pages and in my working life I do often imagine what happens to all the items and ideas from Aero after they move on in the world. I wonder if they have found good homes, if products still satisfy years after they have been purchased. They are gone, but they all exist somewhere new. And I realize that I am one such client of both the studio and the store. The fact is, I buy or design what I would like to have at home. It's the gift of my profession that I can share those inclinations with others.

DEEDS

DEEDS

It seems fitting, therefore, to share a little window into my own home as it is today, with pieces that have come from Aero to fill my house and routines. Some things here will be familiar from earlier pictures, saved and remixed with new finds over the years. Others retire here after being used as models in the studio for new products or residences. And I see how much each of these scenes feels like a continuation of the world of Aero, with shelves like Aero's shelves, the kinds of materials, collections, dualities, that I love to work with. All this is woven into the specific history of my livelihood and my house. All these treasures have navigated their way home.

This is the Aero of now, the me of now. The now of what I think is modern, the now of continuity.

And from the beginning to now, as always, I will go looking for the new thing that wants to be found.

THOMAS O'BRIEN

Academy House

Like the shelves of Aero, the bookcases in my living room are a library of collections and assembled interests—all things that are real and personal to me. The books are organized according to subject: gardens, local history, art, reference. I speak a lot about the idea of living with books and collections because I truly believe that scholarship is an essential part of discovery: no one knows everything when they start collecting, so you learn as you go. Treasures slowly accumulate but these shelves mostly stay as they are, like the memory of a certain gallery in a museum or so many of the shops that I wish still existed, where I knew exactly what they'd have. The feeling for me when I turn to my library is the welcome of what's ancient and favorite.

Upstairs in the guest rooms, Impressionist landscapes and coastlines. Many generations. A peg rack above the stairs, with my childhood flannel cap and young Tessa's swimming goggles. Views back and forth across the Brooklyn Bridge, light and airy. New York itself, hand-painted and colorful. A Gothic hat rack purchased many years ago, forever summery in white.

A downstairs coat rack in the hall off the kitchen, with my boyhood "shopping coat". For years I asked my mother if I could have it. Then on one trip home, there it was in the guest room, waiting for me. I have always been looking and shopping. My accountant and friend Allen Gross says my shopping feeds the store. Rich colors and tartans, white floors and the black doors. The halls and corners of this old schoolhouse are my library of light and dark. The rich and simple, old and even new, or the new that comes from the old, are all things I hold onto.

Traveling objects, finally at home. The memories in things, experiments, ideas, the ones I did not sell. An early Aero stacked wood lamp rests on a battered modern side table that looks more like a country antique. A shagreen box from Donna Karan's first home collection that we sold at Aero many years ago. The favorite old nautical photograph now lives by the bay, in a guest bath. A simple industrial stool, painted shiny in my grammar of black, and a wise owl await at the back stair landing. Eileen Gray's own screen maquette, a treasure, hangs above souvenirs at the sitting room fireplace.

Long Island is a reflective place and really home to me. It is alive with various gardens and cooking. So much springs from the collections and resources here. All goes full circle. My store. My studio. My design life. I always say Aero is about home. Not so much that I make my way here. Aero makes its way from here.

ACKNOWLEDGMENTS

MY BEST

Creating a book is, to me, a really great art project. And this is a book that is in many ways about artistic roots. I dreamed of coming to New York to go to art school, and I arrived here in the city filled with a lot of joy and earnestness and a desire to learn every day. Thirty years later, those feelings still drive me. They are at the heart of what Aero will always be. A place to be a student, a collector, a tinkerer, an enthusiast. To always be creating something new.

This book is also a New York story. I know I've been lucky in New York—at the Cooper Union, in the friends I've made, in my first real job at Polo Ralph Lauren, in the longevity of my store and company. As I write these acknowledgments, I'm reminded of my boss at Polo, Jeff Walker. Jeff had these very handsome engraved cards that he would hand out, which simply said: My Best, Jeff Walker. There was something enchanting about the formality of the gesture, a genuine calling card in a modern age. You never forgot the man or his best if you received one of those cards.

I am always trying to do my best. And so, to my customers, my collaborators, and the many of you on whom I have depended at Aero, I offer you my best and my thanks.

My best to Ralph Lauren, for giving me a path. To Jeff, for pointing the way. To Bill, for starting it with me.

To Laura Resen, for finding each other at the beginning. For the constancy of our friendship. For the decades of photographs and the thread of our history that you have lent to this book. You have been my lens on the world for so many years; we've learned so much together. To the important people you brought to Aero, among them Alan and Gloria Siegel, who became my first clients and Aero's early champions. To my longtime clients and to new ones, who let me create the best environments we can dream of.

To the wonderful Lisa Light, who holds me to my best. You ask as much of yourself as you do of me and you never give up even when I need you to change the words all over again. I rely on your insight, your talent, your friendship, and the weekly barometer of your voice on the phone. I think we are both creatures of the process, and regardless of the time it takes, neither of us will ever accept shortcuts. Thank you, always.

To Michelle Arcila, for your modern eye. I have always connected to you as an artist, and it has been so rewarding to see you flourish, even if it means you are not with us at Aero every day. You take the picture of what is, and how it is, in a way that reminds me of how I see. But the magical edge in your photographs is all your own.

To the editors and patrons who were there at Aero twenty years ago. Every generation is sentimental about its own, even as we change and move ahead in our own lives. Some of you are sadly missed, but we remember you and the adventurous spirit of New York City as it was back then, downtown among the lofts and galleries, and we carry on. Dara Caponigro, Margaret Russell,

Pilar Viladas, Ellen Levine, Pamela Fiori, Sarah Medford, Lou Gropp, Marian McEvoy, Stephen Drucker, Newell Turner, Mayer Rus, Michael Reynolds, Trish Foley, Donna Warner, Liz Tilberis, Anna Wintour, Donna Karan, Giorgio Armani. I must thank you all for believing in me.

To my loyal group at Aero, present and past. You are the protectors of all that I dream of and have tried to build here in this company. It's my daily pleasure that you are also a cast of characters who keep my life so rich, funny, exasperating, real, interesting, and at all on schedule.

To Keith Kancar, my motivator in chief. From intern to salesperson to my Vice President, you rally forces like no one else to get all the work done. You are strong when strength is most needed, insistent where others pause, and you hold the vision of all that this company can be. Thank you for eighteen years and counting.

To Terri Cannon-Nelson, for your grace and calm, still your gifts to Aero after all these years. Kevin O'Sullivan, I depend on your intelligence and character every day as you work on so many things that require exacting research, organization, and diplomacy. In the store I am excited about the road ahead with Matthew de Clementi, one in a long line of special, trusted managers. We have such a shared interest in objects and history. Matthew comes to Aero by way of one of my best leaders, from whom I have learned so much: Julia McFarlane, Soho pioneer and proprietor of one of its first, but not forgotten, home stores, Ad Hoc. Jacqueline Fitzgerald has been with me since Spring Street, one of our old guard but still our leading arbiter of style.

To Peter Iral, for all that you created in your time with Aero. Every best wish on your next adventures. And to Roberto Sosa and all of the studio designers and architects, who work with me as closely

on the design of intricate metalwork fittings as on the plan for a whole house. Thank you for your tireless devotion to detail.

I have many relationships in the world of products and antiques that were born of this store. From the family of workrooms and colleagues who have been with me from the beginning— Jonas Upholstery, Gill and Lagodich, Gary Carlson and Robert Loughlin, Robert Altman, Richard Kazarian—to the partners who have allowed me to make my goods on a larger scale, I am so grateful for the opportunities you have given me to do what I love. My thanks especially to Andy Singer, for his support and interest in the world of vintage modern and industrial design that inspire our lighting business together. This partnership is unique in its magnitude, and it brings me full circle back to the very first products I designed at Aero. Probably nothing comes closer than a good lamp to the core of what Aero is about: that 1930s ideal of engineering, craftsmanship, utility, and decoration, all in one.

My very best to the good people of Abrams Books, who indulge my love of art and print. I'm indebted to you for letting me make my books in this way, really an old-fashioned way. Because at the speed of life today it is ever rarer to be given time to develop an idea into a completely crafted thing that doesn't follow some prescribed formula. Rebecca Kaplan, my steadfast editor, who is always working to keep the sailing smooth; John Gall, who stepped in to design this beautiful book with such perception and modern elegance; Deborah Aaronson, our publisher, who I believe makes amazing books with greater integrity than anyone else.

Finally and mostly, to Dan, for your peace and brilliance. I spent many years drawing my happiness from my work, in what it's meant to me to have this store and all the hard-fought battles of creative life, but you have taught me otherwise. Life with you is easy. It is new, every day. Now my best is really our best. And it is yet to come.

CREDITS

Photography Credits:

Aero: First opening spread, 10, 11, 90, 101 (bottom), 109, 137, 139, 140, 141, 142, 143, 144, 145, 154, 155 (bottom), 156–57, 159, 160 (top left), 160 (bottom), 162, 163, 164, 165, 183, 184-185, 186-187, 188, 189, 191, 192, 193 (left, top and bottom), 194–95, 197, 198, 199, 200, 201, 202, 203, 206 (top left), 207, 210, 211, 212 (top left and bottom right), 213, 214, 215, 237, 246, 247, 249 (top), 251 (left)

Michelle Arcila: 229, 230, 233, 234–35, 236, 237 (bottom), 238–39, 240–41, 242, 243, 244, 245, 248, 249 (bottom), 250, 251 (right), 252, 253, 257, 258–59, 260–61, 262, 263, 264, 265, 266, 267, 268, 269

Laura Resen: 9, 15, 17, 19, 20, 21, 22, 23, 24–25, 26, 27, 28, 29, 31, 33 (top), 36, 37, 39 (left), 40, 41, 42 (top), 43, 53, 54, 55, 62, 63, 64, 65, 67, 68, 70, 71, 72, 73, 74, 75, 76–77, 78–79, 80, 81, 83, 84, 86, 87, 88–89, 91, 94 (top), 95, 96, 97, 98–99, 100 (top), 101 (top), 102–3, 104, 105, 106, 107, 108, 111, 113, 114–15, 116, 117, 119, 120–21, 123, 126–27, 128, 129, 130, 131, 132, 133, 134, 135, 147, 148, 151, 152–53, 155 (top), 158 (top right), 160 (top right), 167, 169, 170, 171, 172–73, 174–75, 176, 177, 178, 179, 181, 190, 193 (top right), 196, 206 (right), 209, 212 (top right), 217, 219, 220, 221, 222, 223, 224–25, 226, 227

Thomas O'Brien: Dedication page, 12, 13, 30, 32, 33 (bottom), 35, 38, 39 (right), 42 (bottom), 45, 46, 47, 48–49, 50–51, 52, 56, 57, 58, 59, 60, 61, 89 (right), 92, 93, 94 (bottom), 100 (bottom), 158 (left, top and bottom), 161, 204–5, 208

Peter Iral: Opposite title page, 254, 255

Endpaper photographs by Michelle Arcila, from Aero's twentieth anniversary celebration, November 14, 2012, in New York City.

Editor: Rebecca Kaplan

Designer: John Gall

Production Manager: Anet Sirna-Bruder

Library of Congress Control Number: 2013935715

ISBN: 978-1-4197-0675-2

Copyright © 2013 Thomas O'Brien

Printed and bound in China

10 9 8 7 6 5 4 3 2 1

Abrams books are available at special discounts when purchased in quantity for premiums and promotions as well as fundraising or educational use. Special editions can also be created to specification. For details, contact specialsales@abramsbooks.com or the address below.

115 West 18th Street
New York, NY 10011
www.abramsbooks.com

Judy Riflea
Dr. Ben Casy

WILLIAM MCINTOSH
4 Union Sq West 1121
NYC 10003

JAMES CHRISPE
156 SPRING
431·8466

EDWARD M. GOW
BALLENA STUDIO
P.O. BOX 47
NY NY 10012

Steven Klein
306 W 13th
NYC 10019

JACK YOUNET
324 W83RD APT SE
NEW YORK N.Y.
10024

Every
ancient
feel like
40. La
the cool
Every
a huge
power

127 Y James
37
164

AERO STUDIOS
132 SPRING STREET NEW YORK CITY 10012
T 966.4700 F 966.4701 | COOPER CLUB CHAIR | SIDE ELEVATION SCALE 1½" = 1' | 6.24.07 GB

Additions to TOB Christmas party 2001

1) Stacey Fisher
Exposure New York
177 Prince Street, 5th Floor
New Y...   10012